HEADSCARVES AND HYMENS

HEADSCARVES AND HYMENS

WHY THE MIDDLE EAST NEEDS A SEXUAL REVOLUTION

MONA ELTAHAWY

FARRAR, STRAUS AND GIROUX   NEW YORK

Farrar, Straus and Giroux
18 West 18th Street, New York 10011

The chapter "Why They Hate Us" was originally published in different form as "Why Do They Hate Us?" in the May–June 2012 issue of *Foreign Policy*.

Grateful acknowledgment is made for permission to reprint an excerpt from the poem "A Litany for Survival" by Audre Lorde. Copyright © 1978, 1995 by Audre Lorde, from *The Black Unicorn* and *The Collected Poems of Audre Lorde*, both published by W. W. Norton. Used herewith by permission of W. W. Norton & Company, Inc., and the Charlotte Sheedy Literary Agency.

The Library of Congress has cataloged the hardcover edition as follows:
Eltahawy, Mona, 1967–
    Headscarves and hymens : why the middle east needs a sexual revolution / Mona Eltahawy.
        pages   cm
    ISBN 978-0-86547-803-9 (hardback) — ISBN 978-0-374-71065-1 (e-book)
    1. Misogyny—Middle East.   2. Sex discrimination against women—Middle East.   3. Women's rights—Middle East.   4. Arab Spring, 2010–   I. Title.

HQ1237.5.M628 E47 2015
323.3'40956—dc23

                                    2014043834

Paperback ISBN: 978-0-374-53665-7

Designed by Abby Kagan

www.fsgbooks.com
www.twitter.com/fsgbooks • www.facebook.com/fsgbooks

10   9   8   7   6

To the girls of the Middle East and North Africa: Be immodest, rebel, disobey, and know you deserve to be free

Write with your eyes like painters, with your ears like musicians, with your feet like dancers. You are the truthsayer with quill and torch. Write with your tongues of fire. Don't let the pen banish you from yourself. Don't let the ink coagulate in your pens. Don't let the censor snuff out the spark, nor the gags muffle your voice. Put your shit on the paper.

We are not reconciled to the oppressors who whet their howl on our grief. We are not reconciled.

—GLORIA ANZALDÚA, "Speaking in Tongues:
A Letter to Third World Women Writers"

CONTENTS

CONTENTS

HEADSCARVES
AND HYMENS

WHY THEY HATE US

In "Distant View of a Minaret," the late and much-neglected Egyptian writer Alifa Rifaat begins her short story with a woman so unmoved during sex with her husband that, as he focuses solely on his pleasure, she notices a spiderweb she must sweep off the ceiling and has time to ruminate on her husband's repeated refusal to prolong intercourse until she climaxes, "as though purposely to deprive her." Just before her husband reaches orgasm, the call to prayer interrupts their intercourse, and he rolls over. After washing up, she loses herself in prayer, and looks out onto the street from her balcony. She interrupts her reverie to dutifully prepare coffee for her husband to drink after his nap. Taking it to their bedroom to pour it in front of him, as he prefers, she notices that he is dead. She instructs their son to go get a doctor. "She returned to the living room and poured out the coffee for herself. She was surprised at how calm she was," Rifaat writes.

In a crisp three and a half pages of fiction, Rifaat lays out a trifecta of sex, death, and religion that forms the pulsating heart of misogyny in the Middle East. Here is a writer who, when she was alive, was held up by academics as an "authentic" Egyptian woman, untainted by a foreign language—she spoke only Arabic—and influence from abroad. It is said that Rifaat never traveled outside Egypt, although she did perform a pilgrimage to Mecca and attended a literary conference in the United Kingdom. She was forced by her family to marry a man of their choice, with whom she traveled across Egypt.

Rifaat does not mince words, nor does she mollify. In the slim volume of short stories titled *Distant View of a Minaret*, she introduces you to a sexually frustrated middle-aged wife who wonders if her mother suffered the same fate with her father, and another mother who laments her youth lost to female genital mutilation and a society that fought her womanhood at every turn. The stories show women constantly sublimating themselves in religion, even as this faith is used against them by clerics and male-dominated society.

There is no sugarcoating it. We Arab women live in a culture that is fundamentally hostile to us, enforced by men's contempt. They don't hate us because of our freedoms, as the tired post-9/11 American cliché had it. We have no freedoms because they hate us, as Rifaat powerfully says.

Yes: They hate us. It must be said.

"The fact is, there's no joy for a girl in growing up, it's just one disaster after another till you end up an old woman who's good for nothing and who's real lucky to find someone to feel sorry for her," Rifaat writes in the story "Bahiyya's Eyes."

Some may ask why I'm bringing this up now, when the Middle East and North Africa are in turmoil, when people are losing their lives by the thousands, when it can sometimes seem as though the revolutions that began in 2010—incited not by the usual hatred of America and Israel, but by a common demand for freedom and dignity—have lost their way. After all, shouldn't everyone receive basic rights first, before women demand special treatment? Also, what does gender or, for that matter, sex have to do with the Arab Spring? It should have everything to do with the revolution. This is our chance to dismantle an entire political and economic system that treats half of humanity like children at best. If not now, when?

Name me an Arab country, and I'll recite a litany of abuses against women occurring in that country, abuses fueled by a toxic mix of culture and religion that few seem willing to disentangle lest they blaspheme or offend. When more than 90 percent of women who have ever married in Egypt have had their genitals cut in the name of "purity," then surely we must all blaspheme. When Egyptian women are subjected to humiliating "virginity tests" merely for speaking out, it's no time for silence. When an article in the Egyptian criminal code says that if a woman has been beaten by her husband "with good intentions," no punitive damages can be obtained, then to hell with political correctness. And what, pray tell, are "good intentions"? They are legally deemed to include any beating that is not "severe" or "directed at the face." What all this means is that when it comes to the status of women in the Arab world, it's not better than you think. It's much, much worse. Even after these "revolutions," women remain covered up and anchored to the home, are denied the simple mobility of getting into their own cars, are forced to get permission from men to travel, and are unable to marry or divorce without a male guardian's blessing.

The Arabic-speaking countries of the Middle East and North Africa stand apart in their terrible record on women's rights. Not a single Arab country ranks in the top one hundred positions on the World Economic Forum's Global Gender Gap Report, putting the region as a whole solidly at the planet's rock bottom. The annual report looks at four key areas: health (life expectancy, etc.), access to education, economic participation (salaries, job types, and seniority), and political engagement. Neighbors Saudi Arabia and Yemen, for instance, are eons apart when it comes to gross domestic product (GDP), but only eight places separate them on the Global Gender Gap Report, with the kingdom at 127 and Yemen coming in at 136, the very bottom of the 2013 index. Morocco, often touted for its "progressive" family law (a 2005 report by Western "experts" called it "an example for Muslim countries aiming to integrate into modern society"), ranks 129th.

It's easy to see why the lowest-ranked country is Yemen, where 49 percent of women are illiterate, 59 percent do not participate in the labor force, and there were no women in parliament as of 2013. Horrific news reports about eight-year-old girls dying on the evening of their "wedding" to much older men have done little to stem the tide of child marriage there. Instead, demonstrations in support of child marriage outstrip those against it, and clerics declare that opponents of state-sanctioned pedophilia are apostates because the Prophet Mohammed, according to them, married his second wife, Aisha, when she was a child.

At least Yemeni women can drive. It surely hasn't ended their problems, but it symbolizes freedom of mobility—and nowhere does such symbolism resonate more than in Saudi Arabia, where child marriage is also practiced and where grown women are treated like children their entire lives, made to obtain the permission of a male guardian to do the most basic of things. Saudi women far outnumber their male counterparts on university campuses but are reduced to watching far less qualified men control every aspect of their lives.

Nothing prepared me for Saudi Arabia. I was born in Egypt, but my family left for London when I was seven years old. After almost eight years in the United Kingdom, we moved to Saudi Arabia in 1982. Both my parents, Egyptians who had earned PhDs in medicine in London, had found jobs in Jeddah, teaching medical students and technicians clinical microbiology. The campuses were segregated. My mother taught the women on the female campus, and my father taught the men on the male campus. When an instructor of the same gender wasn't available, the classes were taught via closed-circuit television, and the students would have to ask questions using telephone sets. My mother, who had been the breadwinner of the family for our last year in the United Kingdom, when we lived in Glasgow, now found that she could not legally drive. We became dependent on my father to take us everywhere. As we waited for our new car to be delivered, we relied on gypsy cabs and public buses. On the buses, we would buy our ticket from the driver, and then my mother and I would make our way to the back two rows (four if we were lucky) designated for women. The back of the bus. What does that remind you of? Segregation is the only way to describe it.

It felt as though we'd moved to another planet whose inhabitants fervently wished women did not exist. I lived in this surreal atmosphere for six years. In this world, women, no matter how young or how old, are required to have a male guardian—a father, a brother, or even a son—and can do nothing without this guardian's permission. Infantilized beyond belief, they cannot travel, open a bank account, apply for a job, or even get medical treatment without a man's stamp of approval. I watched all this with a mounting sense of horror and confusion.

I would mention voting rights, but back when I lived in Saudi Arabia, *no one* could vote. King Abdullah had said women will be allowed to vote and run for office in the 2015 elections, but it remains to be seen if clerics— such as the Grand Mufti of Saudi Arabia, who believes that women's involvement in politics "will open the door to evil"—will scuttle that promise as they did in 2009, when only men were enfranchised in Saudi Arabia's first-ever municipal elections.

Yes, this is Saudi Arabia, the country where a gang-rape survivor was sentenced to jail for agreeing to get into a car with an unrelated male and needed a royal pardon; Saudi Arabia, where a woman who broke the ban on driving was sentenced to ten lashes and, again, needed a royal pardon. So bad is it for women in Saudi Arabia that tiny paternalistic pats on the back—such as the king's promise to give women the vote in 2015—are greeted with acclaim from international observers, and the monarch behind them, King Abdullah, was hailed as a "reformer"—even by those who ought to know better, such as *Newsweek*, which in 2010 named the king one of the top eleven most respected world leaders. This so-called reformer's answer to the revolutions popping up across the region was to numb his people with still more government handouts—especially for the

religious zealots from whom the Saudi royal family in-
hales legitimacy.

When I encountered this country at age fifteen, I was
traumatized into feminism—there's no other way to describe it—because to be a female in Saudi Arabia is to be
the walking embodiment of sin. The kingdom is un-
abashed in its worship of a misogynistic god and never
suffers any consequences for it, thanks to the triple advantage of having oil; being home to Islam's two holiest
places, Mecca and Medina; and controlling the flow of
petrodollars that keep the weapons manufacturers of its
Western allies happily funded.

Then (the 1980s and '90s) as now, clerics on Saudi TV
were obsessed with women and their orifices, especially
what came out of them. I'll never forget hearing that if a
baby boy urinated on you, you could go ahead and pray
in the same clothes, yet if a baby girl peed on you, you
had to change. What on earth made girls' urine impure?
I wondered.

The hatred of women.

This clerical obsession with women's organs continues today. My favorite recent howler: driving will dam-
age your ovaries.

"If a woman drives a car, not out of pure necessity,
that could have negative physiological impacts as func-
tional and physiological medical studies show that it
automatically affects the ovaries and pushes the pelvis
upwards," the Saudi cleric Saleh Lohaidan told the news

website Sabq in 2013. "That is why we find those who regularly drive have children with clinical problems of varying degrees."

Saudi Arabia follows an ultraconservative interpretation of Islam known alternatively as Wahhabism or Salafism, the former associated more directly with the kingdom, and the latter, austere form of Islam with those who live outside Saudi Arabia. The kingdom's petrodollars and concerted proselytizing efforts have taken Wahhabism/Salafism global, and with it the interpretations of Islam that make women's lives in Saudi Arabia little short of prison sentences.

Yet the hatred of women is not unique to Salafism. It is not merely a Saudi phenomenon, a hateful curiosity of a rich, isolated desert. The Islamist hatred of women burns brightly across the region—now more than ever. By "Islamists," I intend the Associated Press's definition: "An advocate or supporter of a political movement that favors reordering government and society in accordance with laws prescribed by Islam." This includes the Muslim Brotherhood, Salafi groups who belong to the Sunni sect of Islam, and the Shiite militias in Iraq.

The obsession with controlling women and our bodies often stems from the suspicion that, without restraints, women are just a few degrees short of sexual insatiability. Take as an example the words of Yusuf al-Qaradawi, the popular Egyptian cleric; resident of Doha, Qatar; and longtime conservative TV host on Al Jazeera. Al-Qaradawi supported the revolutions, no doubt hoping they would eliminate the tyrants who had long tormented and oppressed both him and the Muslim Brotherhood movement from which he springs. While al-Qaradawi, who commands a huge audience on and off the satellite channels, may say that female genital mutilation (which he calls "circumcision," a common euphemism that tries to put the practice on a par with male circumcision) is not "obligatory," you will also find the following priceless observation in one of his books: "I personally support this under the current circumstances in the modern world. Anyone who thinks that circumcision is the best way to protect his daughters should do it," he writes, adding, "The moderate opinion is in favor of practicing circumcision to reduce temptation." So even among "moderates," girls' genitals are cut to ensure that their sexual desire is nipped in the bud. Al-Qaradawi has since issued a fatwa against female genital mutilation (FGM), but it came as no surprise that when Egypt banned the practice in 2008, some Muslim Brotherhood legislators opposed the law. Upholding the credo of the Muslim Brotherhood, to which al-Qaradawi belongs, several of the movement's women are on record as supporting or legitimizing FGM, including Azza el-Garf (a former member of parliament) and Mohamed Morsi's women's affairs adviser during his brief presidency, who called FGM a form of "beautificiation."

Yet while clerics busy themselves suppressing female

desire, it is the men who can't control themselves. On the streets of too many countries in the region, sexual harassment is epidemic. In a 2008 survey by the Egyptian Center for Women's Rights, more than 80 percent of Egyptian women said they'd experienced sexual harassment, and more than 60 percent of men admitted to harassing women. A 2013 UN survey reported that 99.3 percent of Egyptian women experience street sexual harassment. Men grope and sexually assault us, and yet we are blamed for it because we were in the wrong place at the wrong time, wearing the wrong thing. Cairo has women-only subway cars to "protect" us from wandering hands and worse; countless Saudi malls are for families only, barring single men from entry unless they produce a requisite female to accompany them. Families impose curfews on their daughters so that they're not raped or assaulted, and yet is anyone telling boys and men not to rape or assault us?

We often hear how the Middle East's failing economies have left many men unable to marry, and some even use this fact to explain rising levels of sexual harassment on the streets. Yet we never hear how a later marriage age affects women. Do women have sex drives or not? Apparently, the Arab jury is still out on the basics of human biology. Here is some more wisdom from al-Qaradawi: virgins must be "patient" and resist the temptation of masturbation, which he claims is "more dangerous" than male masturbation because if a virgin

inserts her fingers or other objects into her vaginal opening, she could perforate her hymen and her family and
future husband will think she committed fornication by
having sex before marriage.

Enter that call to prayer and the sublimation through
religion that Rifaat so brilliantly introduces in her story.
Just as regime-appointed clerics lull the poor across the
region with promises of justice in the next world, rather
than a reckoning with the corruption and nepotism of
the dictator in this life, so women are silenced by men
who use women's faith to imprison them.

In Kuwait, where Islamists fought women's enfranchisement for years, the four women elected to parliament
in 2009 were hounded by conservatives, who demanded
that the two female parliamentarians who didn't cover
their hair wear headscarves. When the Kuwaiti parliament was dissolved in December 2011, an Islamist parliamentarian demanded that the new house (one devoid
of a single female legislator) discuss his proposed "decent attire" law. It did not become law, but the obsession
with women's bodies continued. In May 2014, *The Washington Post* reported that an Islamist member of Kuwait's
parliament, who is head of the committee for "combating
alien behavior," said the committee had approved his
proposal to ban female "nudity" at places accessible to
the public, including swimming pools and hotels. The
lawmaker refused to define what he meant by "nudity."
At the time of writing, the proposal had still to be ap-

proved by Kuwait's National Assembly and government, but it had already created a political standoff as one lawmaker, Nabil al-Fadl, said he would resign if the assembly approved the proposal, which he described as a "regression," according to the Kuwaiti daily newspaper *al-Shahed*.

Whatever the fate of the bill, the obsession with women's bodies has serious ramifications. The *Gulf News* reported that just days before the "bikini ban" proposal, a Kuwaiti woman lost a custody battle with her ex-husband after his lawyer showed the court a picture of her wearing a bikini in the company of another man while abroad.

"The mother cannot be trusted to raise the children properly and the picture as an example indicates a lack of modesty and a deficiency in her morals that erode trust in her and result in public disdain as society assesses her actions morally or religiously," the lawyer said.

In Libya, after a revolution that brought to an end forty-two years of absolute rule by Muammar al-Qaddafi, the first thing the head of the interim government, Mustafa Abdel Jalil, promised to do was lift the late Libyan tyrant's restrictions on polygamy. Lest you think Muammar al-Qaddafi was a feminist of any kind, remember that under his rule, girls and women who survived sexual assaults or were suspected of "moral crimes" were dumped into "social rehabilitation centers," effectively prisons from which they could not leave unless a man agreed to marry them or their families took them back. Human Rights Watch reports that even after the overthrow of Qaddafi, many women still were being sent to "social rehabilitation" centers by their families "for no other reason than that they had been raped, and were then ostracized for 'staining their family's honor.'"

The return to polygamy in Libya (where, as of 2013, men can take additional wives against their first wife's will, according to *Al Arabiya News*) is particularly shameful because female demonstrators played a critical role in the Libyan revolution. Two days before protests planned to emulate the uprisings in neighbors Tunisia and Egypt, female relatives of prisoners who had been killed by Qaddafi's forces in the 1996 Abu Salim prison massacre protested the detention of the attorney representing them against the Qaddafi regime. The women's protests inspired fellow Libyans in the eastern province of Benghazi to join them, and from there the demonstrations grew into a nationwide uprising.

Egypt's first parliamentary elections after the start of its revolution were dominated by men stuck in the seventh century. Only 984 women contested seats, compared with 8,415 men. A quarter of parliamentary seats were claimed by Salafis, whose belief in a woman's rights basically begins and ends with her "right" to wear the niqab, a full-face veil. When fielding female candidates, Egypt's Salafi Nour Party superimposed an image of a flower on each woman's face in campaign materials.

Women are not to be seen or heard; even their voices are a temptation.

Flowers instead of women's faces, in the middle of a revolution in Egypt! A revolution in which women were killed, beaten, shot at, and sexually assaulted while fighting alongside men to rid our country of Mubarak— and yet so many patriarchs still oppress us. The Muslim Brotherhood, which held almost half the total seats in the revolutionary parliament before it was dissolved by the Supreme Court, does not believe that a woman (or a Christian, for that matter) should be president. The woman who headed the "women's committee" of the Brotherhood's political party has said that women should not march or protest because it's more "dignified" to let their husbands and brothers demonstrate for them.

It was in Egypt, too, that less than a month after President Hosni Mubarak stepped down, the military junta that replaced him, ostensibly to "protect the revolution," detained dozens of male and female activists after it cleared Tahir Square. Tyrants oppress, beat, and torture all, we know. Yet reserved for female activists were "virginity tests": rapes disguised as a medical doctor inserting his finger into the vaginal opening in search of an intact hymen.

This is where the soldiers in our regimes and the men on our streets unite: they both sexually assault women to remind us that public space is a male prerogative. Security forces and civilians alike violated women in Tahrir

Square, and men of the revolution—be they from the left or the right—have set us back with their insistence that "women's issues" cannot dominate "revolutionary politics." Yet I ask: Whose revolution?

Lest you think it's just Islamists such as the Muslim Brotherhood or the Salafists of Saudi Arabia whose misogyny runs roughshod over our rights, remember that the Muslim Brotherhood's Mohamed Morsi, the narrow victor of Egypt's first presidential elections after Mubarak's ouster, was himself ousted by the ostensibly secular defense minister Abdel-Fattah el-Sisi. El-Sisi presented himself (especially to women) as the man who saved Egypt from a terror-filled regression to the Dark Ages at the hands of the Muslim Brotherhood. Anyone foolish enough to believe that would do well to remember that el-Sisi approved of those "virginity tests" the military enforced on female activists.

That is why I blame a toxic mix of culture and religion. Whether our politics are tinged with religion or with military rule, the common denominator is the oppression of women.

Tunisia, first to rise up against its tyrant and first to push him out, emanates the brightest glimmer of hope, but it still has far to go. Tunisian women held their breath after the Islamist Ennahda Party won the largest share of votes in the country's Constituent Assembly in 2011. Subsequently, female university professors and students reported facing assaults and intimidation from Islamists for not wearing headscarves.

In March 2014, I went to Tunisia with the producer Gemma Newby to interview women for our radio documentary *The Women of the Arab Spring* for the BBC World Service. Among the women I spoke with were some who had helped draft the new constitution, including a secular lawmaker, a lawmaker from the Ennahda Party, and activists who had lobbied for the strongest possible pro-woman language in the document. Although it remains to be seen whether their efforts will translate into more than words on paper, thanks to them, Tunisia's constitution is the first in the Arab world that recognizes men and women as equals. Unlike their counterparts in that first parliament in Egypt after the revolution, not all female Islamist lawmakers in Tunisia's Constituent Assembly are foot soldiers of the patriarchy.

Some of Ennhada's female lawmakers opposed the language on equality in Tunisia's constitution. Yet, due to the efforts of others, such as Fatoum Elaswad, who insisted on working with her secular counterparts, it passed.

"When women fight, only men benefit," she told me.

There is a lesson there.

My own feminist revolution evolved slowly, and traveled the world with me. To this day I have no idea what dissident professor or librarian placed feminist texts on the bookshelves at the university library in Jeddah, but I found them there. They filled me with terror. I understood they were pulling at a thread that would unravel everything. Now that I'm older, I can see that feeling terrified is how you recognize what you need. Terror encourages you to jump, even when you don't know if you'll ever land.

Before I found those books, I was depressed and suffocated by Saudi ultraconservatism but could not find the words to express my frustration at how religion and culture were being used as a double whammy against women. Those books helped me formulate questions I continue to ask to this day, questions that have made me the woman I am.

I discovered feminist writings from all over the world, but even more significantly, I discovered that the Middle East had a feminist heritage of its own; it was not imported from the "West," as opponents of women's rights sometimes claim. There was Huda Shaarawi, a feminist who launched Egypt's women's rights movement and who publicly removed her face veil in Cairo in 1923; Doria Shafik, who led fifteen hundred women as they stormed the Egyptian parliament in the 1950s and then staged a hunger strike for women's enfranchisement; Nawal El Saadawi, an Egyptian physician, writer, and activist;

Fatima Mernissi, a Moroccan sociologist—all fierce advocates of women's rights. They gave me a new language to describe what I was seeing all around me. I told my parents I could not survive in Jeddah, and made plans to study in Cairo.

What would have happened if my family had stayed in the United Kingdom and not moved to Saudi Arabia? Would I have become a feminist? Would the anger that burns in me to this day have been ignited?

I was exposed to yet more injustice when I moved to Egypt. To step outside the house where I was living with my uncle and aunt was to witness poverty on a shocking scale. Every girl living on the streets reminded me of the two-year-old sister I'd left behind in Saudi Arabia, and just how vastly different their lives were. The university I enrolled in, the American University in Cairo, was a bubble of privilege that only set in stark relief the ugliness of the poverty around me. I would take a public bus from the lower-middle-class neighborhood where I lived and an hour later I would be with people who'd been chauffeured for most of their lives. It was a crash course in Egypt's classist society; many of my classmates acted as if there were no one suffering on the streets their chauffeured cars passed through.

One of my professors was a columnist for a privately owned English-language paper called *The Middle East Times*, which had to publish in Cyprus because it was denied a license to print in Egypt. I started to freelance for the paper in 1989, reporting on human rights and women's issues. One of my assignments took me to the launch of that year's annual report from the Egyptian Organization for Human Rights, an outfit of courageous activists who exposed torture under the Mubarak regime and advocated for victims of his police state. I met a woman in her sixties whose story has stayed with me ever since. It showed me that revolutions are long in the making; their roots embrace many people and causes.

The woman had come to Cairo from her home in southern Egypt because her neighbors had told her that there was a group in the capital who could help her find justice. She went to the Egyptian Organization for Human Rights and told them that she ran a kiosk that sold soda and cigarettes. One day, police insisted she testify against a "car thief." She refused, saying she didn't know of any "car thief" and so could not bear false testimony against one. She told the organization that the police then dragged her to the precinct, where they sodomized her with the leg of a chair.

I took home with me the annual report in which her story was included. The uncle I was living with—a physician, an educated man who followed the news and had traveled—asked to read it. He returned it to me the next morning, shaking his head. "This happens in Egypt?" was all he could say.

Many Egyptians assumed that if they kept their backs to the wall and weren't overtly political they would survive. To hear a story like this woman's reminds us of the countless others who did not survive and who never got to tell their story—such as the thirteen-year-old boy arrested for selling tea bags who was allegedly so brutally tortured by the police that the coroner conducting the autopsy sobbed as he documented the boy's wounds. How many countless, invisible victims of arbitrary police brutality were there in Egypt? How many young people—the majority of the population in Egypt, as they are in the rest of the Middle East and North Africa—felt they had no future, economically or politically? How long before the people would rise up and demand justice? "Where is the revolution?" I would ask my aunts and uncles every day.

Twenty-three years later, in January 2011, people by the hundreds of thousands marched on Tahrir Square. I was living in the United States by then. I did not have enough money to fly back to Egypt, so I decided to do what I could for the revolution from New York City. I lived in television and radio stations, sleeping sometimes just an hour or two between "hits" (media appearances) in which I reminded U.S. television networks that five American administrations had supported Mubarak's regime at the expense of the liberty and dignity of the Egyptian people, those same people they were now watching on their television screens rise up and demand, "Bread, Liberty, Social Justice, Human Dignity!" I persuaded CNN to remove "Chaos in Egypt" as their banner headline and replace it with "Uprising in Egypt," after I made an impassioned appeal for them to see what was happening as a protest against oppression. This was a revolution—and it had been long in the making.

As events unfolded, I watched hours and hours of video footage on YouTube, touching the screen as though it would connect me to the life force I was seeing on the streets in Cairo. Here was the revolution, finally!

But for women, there have always been two revolutions to undertake: one fought with men against regimes that oppress everyone, and a second against the misogyny that pervades the region. As jubilant as I was to see a dictator toppled in Egypt and in other countries in the region, and as thrilled as I am to see those countries stumble toward democracy, however clumsily—what else to expect after so many years of oppression?—I am still painfully aware that although women may have been on the barricades beside men, they are in danger of losing what few rights they had in postrevolutionary Egypt and in Tunisia, Libya, Yemen, and Syria.

A 2013 Thomson Reuters Foundation poll surveying twenty-two Arab states placed three out of five countries in which revolutions had started in the bottom five positions for women's rights. Egypt was judged to be the single worst country for women's rights, scoring badly in almost every category, including gender violence, reproductive rights, treatment of women in the family, and female inclusion in politics and the economy. The Muslim

Brotherhood's rise to power, culminating with the election of President Mohamed Morsi, posed a significant challenge to gender equality. Since Morsi's ouster by the military, however, we have been reminded that neither Islamists nor the armed forces were great friends of women's rights—remember the "virginity tests."

The Reuters poll found dismal circumstances in the other countries undergoing revolutions. In Syria, rights groups say that forces loyal to President Bashar al-Assad have targeted women with rape and torture, while hardline Islamists have stripped them of rights in rebel-held territory.

In Libya, experts voiced concern over the spread of armed militias and a rise in kidnapping, extortion, random arrests, and physical abuse of women. They said that the uprising had failed to enshrine women's rights in law.

It was in the "new Egypt" that I was sexually assaulted by security forces during clashes on Mohamed Mahmoud Street in November 2011—beaten so severely that my left arm and right hand were broken—and detained, first by the Ministry of the Interior and then by military intelligence, for some twelve hours, two of which I spent blindfolded. Only by virtue of a borrowed cell phone was I able to send an alert on Twitter about my situation. At least twelve other women were subjected to various forms of sexual assault during the protest in which riot police attacked me. None of them has spoken publicly about her ordeal, likely due to shame or family pressure. In December 2011, the whole world saw the photograph of the woman who became the icon of state-sanctioned abuse, stripped down to her blue bra as soldiers smashed their feet into her exposed rib cage. Lazily described as "Blue Bra Girl," she became my Unknown Comrade—to this day we don't know her name; women's rights activists tell me her family has prevented her from speaking about what happened—and she inspired thousands of Egyptian women and men to march against sexual assault. The protest garnered the one and only apology so far from the ruling military junta.

And then? Nothing, really. At the first anniversary of the Mohamed Mahmoud clashes—with Mohamed Morsi of the Muslim Brotherhood as president—women protesters reported that they were groped by their male counterparts as they tried to escape the security forces' tear gas and pellets. What goes through the mind of a protester who is dodging security forces, tear gas, and blows but nonetheless pauses to grope the body of a fellow protester? Morsi remained silent as organized gangs raped and sexually assaulted women at protests with impunity. On the second anniversary of January 25, at least nineteen women were sexually assaulted, including one who was raped with a knife. All this aimed to punish women for activism and to push them out of public space. And it would not have happened unless there were societal acceptance of such assaults; it would not have happened if women did not face various kinds of sexual violence on a daily basis. It would not have happened if hatred of women had not, for so long, been allowed to breathe and stretch and run so freely in our societies.

In May 2012, I published an article titled "Why Do They Hate Us?" in *Foreign Policy* magazine. The reaction the article generated—by turns supportive, laudatory, and outraged—made it clear that misogyny in the Arab world is an explosive issue.

When I write or give lectures about gender inequality in the Middle East and North Africa, I understand I am walking into a minefield. On one side stands a bigoted and racist Western right wing that is all too eager to hear critiques of the region and of Islam that it can use against us. I would like to remind these conservatives that no country is free of misogyny, and that their efforts to reverse hard-earned women's reproductive rights makes them brothers-in-hatred to our Islamists.

On the other side stand those Western liberals who rightly condemn imperialism and yet are blind to the cultural imperialism they are performing when they silence critiques of misogyny. They behave as if they want to save my culture and faith from me, and forget that they are immune to the violations about which I speak. Blind to the privilege and the paternalism that drive them, they give themselves the right to determine what is "authentic" to my culture and faith. If the right wing is driven by a covert racism, the left sometimes suffers from an implicit racism through which it usurps my right to determine what I can and cannot say.

Culture evolves, but it will remain static if outsiders consistently silence criticism in a misguided attempt to save us from ourselves. Cultures evolve through dissent and robust criticism from their members. When Westerners remain silent out of "respect" for foreign cultures, they show support only for the most conservative elements of those cultures. Cultural relativism is as much my enemy as the oppression I fight within my culture and faith.

One of the criticisms of my essay was that it was written in English. No one ever brings that up as a criticism with regard to articles that expose human rights violations or the failing economies in our region. The double standard is clear: when it comes to women's issues, keep it between us, in a language only "we" can understand, so you don't make us look bad.

Implicit in the criticism of my essay was the charge that I want "the West" to "rescue us." Only we can rescue ourselves. I have never implored anyone else to rescue us from misogyny; it is our fight to win. I implore allies of the countries in this part of the world to pay more attention to women's rights and to refuse to allow cultural relativism to justify horrendous violations of women's rights. This is very different from calling on anyone to "rescue us."

I insist on the right to critique both my culture and my faith in ways that I would reject from an outsider. I expose misogyny in my part of the world to connect the feminist struggle in the Middle East and North Africa to the global one. Misogyny has not been completely wiped out anywhere. Rather, it resides on a spectrum, and our best hope for eradicating it globally is for each of us to expose and to fight against local versions of it, in the understanding that by doing so we advance the global struggle. When I travel and give lectures abroad and I'm asked how best to help women in my part of the world, I say, help your own community's women fight misogyny. By doing so, you help the global struggle against the hatred of women. I have written this book in that spirit; it is my flag, my manifesto that exposes misogyny in my part of the world as a way to connect to that global feminist struggle. Those countries that have managed to reduce their levels of misogyny were not created more respectful of women's rights. Rather, women in these countries have fought hard to expose systemic violations and to liberate women from them.

I have written this book at a time when more and more women of color are speaking out about misogyny and refusing to be quiet for fear of "making us look bad." Black, Latina, and Asian women from the United

States have had to contend with multiple levels of discrimination—racism toward their communities and misogyny from within and without. For too long they were told that exposing the misogyny they face from within would arm the racists who already demonize the men of their communities. For their reckoning with this balancing act, I am grateful for the Black feminist bell hooks, the Black lesbian poet and activist Audre Lorde, and the Chicana feminist thinker Gloria Anzaldúa. Their work, which I quote frequently, gave me the foundation upon which to fight racism and sexism without fear of embarrassing my community.

While I am acutely aware of Islamophobes and xeno-phobic political right-wingers who are all too glad to hear how badly Muslim men treat their women, I'm also acutely aware that there's a right wing among Muslim men that does propagate misogyny. We must confront both, not ally ourselves with one in order to fight the other.

One of the most effective ways to do this is to listen to the voices of women from within the culture who are trying to dismantle misogyny. The women featured throughout these chapters, whose voices are part of the revolution and are essential to ensuring its success, are from within the culture, and they must be heard. The women fighting for the double revolution we need are the direct descendants of our feminist foremothers—of Huda Shaarawi, of Doria Shafik, and of the countless others whose names we might not know but whose struggles to liberate us from a host of misogynies we continue to honor. We stand on the shoulders of these women, and we must fortify our own shoulders for those to come.

I am angry for all the hundreds of thousands of other women who continue to be violated in ways much worse than I was, and who yet have no platform for sharing their experience. I want to move beyond my privilege to remember the millions of women who have none. I know nothing frightens Islamists and the equally misogynistic secular men of our societies more than the demand for women's rights and sexual freedoms—and that is ultimately what our double revolution must achieve.

Why do those men hate us? They hate us because they need us, they fear us, they understand how much control it takes to keep us in line, to keep us good girls with our hymens intact until it's time for them to fuck us into mothers who raise future generations of misogynists to forever fuel their patriarchy. They hate us because we are at once their temptation and their salvation from that patriarchy, which they must sooner or later realize hurts them, too. They hate us because they know that once we rid ourselves of the alliance of State and Street that works in tandem to control us, we will demand a reckoning.

The battles over women's bodies can be won only by a revolution of the mind. Too often women are scolded for daring to bring up "identity politics," and are urged to lay aside "women's rights" for the larger goal of solidarity or fidelity to the revolution. This is a mistake. Huge swaths of the Arab world are being remade now, with far-reaching and unguessed-at repercussions, and women and men both have an unprecedented opportunity to confront, and root out, the systemic hatred of women that reduces us to little more than our headscarves and our hymens.

We might have removed Hosni Mubarak in Egypt, Zine al-Abidine Ben Ali in Tunisia, Muammar al-Qaddafi in Libya, and Ali Abdullah Saleh in Yemen, but until the rage shifts from the oppressors in our presidential palaces to the oppressors on our streets and in our homes—unless we topple the Mubaraks in our mind, in our bedrooms, and on our street corners—our revolution has not even begun.

BLACK VEIL, WHITE FLAG

At Cairo station one spring day in 1923, a crowd of women with veils and long, black cloaks descended from their horse-drawn carriages to welcome home two friends returning from an international feminist meeting in Rome. Huda Shaarawi and Saiza Nabarawi stepped out on to the running board of the train. Suddenly Huda—followed by Saiza, the younger of the two—drew back the veil from her face. The waiting women broke into loud applause. Some imitated the act. Contemporary accounts observed how the eunuchs guarding the women frowned with displeasure. This daring act signaled the end of the harem system in Egypt. At that moment, Huda stood between two halves of her life—one conducted within the conventions of the harem system and the one she would lead at the head of a women's movement.

—FROM THE INTRODUCTION BY MARGOT BADRAN TO
HAREM YEARS: THE MEMOIRS OF AN EGYPTIAN FEMINIST,
BY HUDA SHAARAWI, TRANSLATED BY MARGOT BADRAN

One afternoon in the early 1990s, when I was in my mid-twenties, I sat in the women's carriage on the

Cairo metro. I was wearing one of my favorite skirts: flowers in vivid red and green on a brown background with a matching brown blouse and a beige headscarf with red trim. I took great pride in matching my headscarves to the clothes I wore, and I would have none of the austerity that stamped itself on women in Saudi Arabia, where headscarves and cloaks, known as abayas, were black. My mother and I both refused to wear black headscarves in Saudi Arabia, and I continued that tradition in Egypt, where, thankfully, black was not de rigueur among those of us who wore the hijab, a form of dress that covers everything but the face and hands.

A woman wearing a niqab (a veil, usually black, that covers all of the face apart from the eyes) struck up a conversation with me. "Why aren't you wearing a niqab?" she asked me. Her question was chilling; I'd always found the niqab terrifying in the way it rendered the face and the individual invisible.

"Isn't what I'm wearing enough?" I asked the woman.

"If you want to eat a piece of candy, would you choose one that is in a wrapper or an unwrapped one?" the woman in the niqab asked me.

"I'm a woman, not a piece of candy," I replied.

Candy in a wrapper, a diamond ring in a box—these analogies are commonly used in Egypt and other countries to try to convince women of the value of veiling. They compare women to objects that are precious but devalued by exposure, objects that need to be hidden, protected, and secured. When it comes to what are described as the Islamic restrictions on women's dress, women are never simply women.

There are various explanations for why women veil themselves. Some do it out of piety, believing that the Qur'an mandates this expression of modesty. Others do it because they want to be visibly identifiable as "Muslim," and for them a form of veiling is central to that identity. For some women, the veil is a way to avoid expensive fashion trends and visits to the hair salon. For others, it is a way to be left alone and afforded a bit more freedom to move about in a public space that has become increasingly male-dominated. In recent decades, as veiling became more prevalent throughout the Arab world, the pressure on women who were not veiled began to increase, and more women took on the veil to avoid being harassed on the streets. Some women fought their families for the right to veil, while others were forced to veil by their families. For yet others, it was a way to rebel against the regime or the West.

So the act of wearing the hijab is far from simple. It is burdened with meanings: oppressed woman, pure woman, conservative woman, strong woman, asexual woman, uptight woman, liberated woman. I chose to wear the hijab at the age of sixteen and chose to stop wearing it when I was twenty-five. It is no exaggeration to say that the hijab has consumed a large portion of my intellectual and emotional energy since I first put on a headscarf. I might have stopped wearing one, but I never stopped wrestling with what veiling means for Muslim women. Because I have been open about the fact that I wore the hijab for nine years, I often hear from younger women who are struggling with their veil, and frequently with their families, who insist they continue to wear it: "How did you take it off?" "How did you handle family pressure?" "Do you think it's an obligation?" "Would you ever wear it again?" "My mother has threatened to lock me up at home if I ever take mine off."

Hijab is an Arabic word meaning "barrier" or "partition," but it has come to represent complex principles of modesty and dress. The argument for the hijab begins with this passage from the Qur'an:

> And tell the believing women to reduce [some] of their vision and guard their private parts and not expose their adornment except that which [necessarily] appears thereof and to wrap [a portion of] their headcovers over their chests and not expose their adornment except to their husbands, their fathers, their husbands' fathers, their sons, their husbands' sons, their brothers, their brothers' sons, their sisters' sons, their women, that which their right hands possess, or those male attendants having no physical desire, or children who are not yet aware of the private aspects of women. (sura 24:31)

This interpretation of the Qur'an's instructions on modesty is supported with Hadith literature in which Muhammad is said to have instructed women to cover all of their body except for the face and hands. The Hadith (meaning "tradition") is a collection of sayings and stories attributed to Muhammad and based on oral narratives collected a few centuries after his death. The Bukhari Hadith, considered to be the most authoritative, shows women responding to the Prophet's teaching by covering themselves, supporting the conviction that veiling is Muhammad's direct command.

But veiling has never and will never be as simple as these passages seem to suggest. I didn't realize this when I first began to wear the hijab. It was when I began to struggle with the hijab that I found alternative interpretations—I did not at first have the power or courage simply to stop wearing my headscarf. I needed allies whose religious knowledge I could use against those scholars who maintained that the hijab was religiously mandated.

I found one such alternative in the writings of the Moroccan sociologist and feminist Fatima Mernissi, one of the first intellectual mentors of my feminism. She offered a different interpretation of the Qur'anic verses that contain the word *hijab*, in which she takes the word to mean "a curtain." Reading her books *The Veil and the Male Elite: A Feminist Interpretation of Women's Rights in Islam* and *Beyond the Veil: Male-Female Dynamics in Modern Muslim Societies* offered a lifeline that emboldened me in my independence of thought against the male-dominated mainstream of religious teaching.

Mernissi believed that the "hijab" the Qur'an mentions is meant to indicate a curtain hung to provide privacy for the Prophet and his family. The verse was revealed, Mernissi wrote, after an incident in which guests lingered during a visit to the Prophet and a new wife and Muhammad was too shy to ask the guests to leave his small home. Hijab was never meant to segregate men from women—just to provide privacy for the Prophet and his family—and it was not about concealing women behind veils, either, according to Mernissi. To a young woman struggling with forces she believed she could not stand up to, Mernissi's words were much-needed ammunition.

"All the monotheistic religions are shot through by the conflict between the divine and the feminine, but none more so than Islam, which has opted for the occultation of the feminine, at least symbolically, by trying to veil it, to hide it, to mask it," Mernissi writes in *The Veil and the Male Elite*. "This almost phobic attitude toward women is all the more surprising since we have seen that the prophet has encouraged his adherents to renounce it as representative of the jahiliyya (pre-Islamic period, literally age of ignorance) and its superstitions . . . Is it possible that the hijab, the attempt to veil women, that is claimed today to be basic to Muslim identity, is nothing but the expression of the persistence of the pre-Islamic mentality . . . ?"

I learned from reading the work of Leila Ahmed, an Egyptian American scholar and chair of the Harvard Divinity School, that veiling was prevalent in pre-Islamic society, and not just in Arabia but also in Mediterranean and Mesopotamian civilizations that predated Christianity. It was used, among other things, to differentiate between free women (who veiled) and enslaved women (who did not).

Ahmed further bolstered my ammunition against the hijab by explicitly differing with the opinions that claim the Qur'an mandates veiling. "It is nowhere explicitly prescribed in the Qur'an; the only verses dealing with women's clothing . . . instruct women to guard their private parts and throw a scarf over their bosoms," Ahmed wrote in *Women and Gender in Islam: Historical Roots of a Modern Debate.*

Ahmed emphasizes that during the Prophet's time, veiling was practiced mostly by his wives, as a way of differentiating them from other women. Known as Mothers of the Believers, they were taken as role models of "purity" and decency, and that is one way that veiling became associated with Islamic identity and those virtues in particular. Reading Mernissi and Ahmed was a balm that emboldened me in my struggles with the hijab, and to this day, I often recommend them to younger women undergoing their own struggles.

But the headscarves in the title of this book and the headscarves in this chapter are not simply religious symbols. These days I am less interested in debating the religious necessity of veiling and more interested in asking what the widespread adoption of the hijab has done to the perception of women and to women's perceptions of themselves. Are we more than our headscarves?

Though comprehensive statistics on veiling have not been tabulated, observation suggests that more women in the Middle East and North Africa wear the veil now than at any time since the early decades of the twentieth century. In a 2007 article, *The New York Times* claimed that up to 90 percent of Muslim women in Egypt wear some kind of headscarf. A recent study from the University of Michigan's Institute for Social Research surveyed the Muslim-majority countries of Egypt, Iraq, Lebanon, Pakistan, Saudi Arabia, Tunisia, and Turkey and found that a median 44 percent of respondents preferred that women cover their hair in public. A median 10 percent preferred forms of veiling that covered the body from head to toe, and almost completely covered the face, such as the burqa and the niqab. In Saudi Arabia, that figure rose to 63 percent.

The prevalence of veiling in the Middle East and North Africa today is the latest swing of a pendulum. These shifts from conservative to liberal dress and back again have often been described as motions between "Islam" and the "West," a dichotomy that makes it especially hard to talk about veiling or to critique it without having to choose one or the other. But we must find a way to talk about the hijab that does not frame it as a choice between cultures.

Huda Shaarawi's historic unveiling in 1923, which began a decades-long movement away from the hijab in Egypt, is usually framed in this Islam-versus-the-West dynamic. Shaarawi belonged to the upper class—affluent, and conversant in more languages than just Arabic—which along with a growing middle class, admired European ways and considered them a "modern" blueprint.

Europeans had served as liberal models for the Egyptian intelligentsia since the nineteenth century. In 1899, reformer Qasim Amin wrote a book called *Tahrir al-Mar'a* (*The Liberation of Women*) in which he controversially argued that the veil stood in the way of women's progress and, by extension, Egypt's. Muslim scholars reacted strongly to Amin's polemic and demanded that women who removed their veils be imprisoned or at least fined. They positioned the veil as the "traditional" and "authentic" dress for women, making it the uniform for the less-advantaged for whom education, foreign languages, and European ways were not options.

When Amin's ideas were championed by Evelyn Baring, the British consul general of Egypt, a terrible dynamic was set in place in which women's rights became the cat's-paw of imperial power, making it almost impossible for those opposed to the occupation and to European influence to critique the veil without looking as if they were taking the side of the West.

After the 1952 coup—in which a group of military officers overthrew the king—put an end to the monarchy in Egypt and ended British occupation, unveiling became less associated with the former rulers and closely identified with Egypt's urban female workforce, employed by an expanding public sector. By the 1960s, headscarves were mostly worn only by members of the Muslim Brotherhood movement and in smaller towns and rural parts of Egypt.

So what changed? What made the pendulum swing back to veiling?

Islamist influence grew throughout the Arab world following Israel's humiliating defeat of the Arabs in 1967. In 1979 the Iranian Revolution tantalized the region with the vision of an Islamic state. Also, worsening economies throughout the Arab world drove many workers to seek employment in Saudi Arabia, where they were influenced by Wahhabism. When the workers returned to their homelands, they brought these new conservative beliefs back with them, including more stringent expectations of female modesty.

Anwar Sadat coddled the Islamists in Egypt, using them against internal political enemies. After Islamist army officers assassinated Sadat in 1981, the Mubarak regime, which claimed to be secular, fought its conservative rivals—including the Muslim Brotherhood, Mubarak's most organized opponents—with a conservatism of its own. This is a popular pattern that governments—especially those close to the United States and Europe, such as Egypt's under Sadat and Mubarak—use to protect themselves against charges of being godless or faithless. Conservative clerics appeared on television and other media in a flexing of fundamentalist muscle designed to show that the Muslim Brotherhood did not hold the copyright on piety. A drove of clerics, some state-approved, others not, used cassette tapes and later satellite television channels to get their conservative messages across.

When it came to women, their main message was "Cover up." In the 1990s the populist cleric Omar Abdel Kafi produced cassette tapes advocating the hijab that were bought by Cairo's upper-class women. (Cassette tapes were a way to reach a wide audience while avoiding state censorship, much in the way that social media operate today.) Omar Abdel Kafi is said to have single-handedly "converted" several popular actresses away from the "sinful life" of the screen to the piety of the veil, thereby setting an example for their fans.

With the advent of satellite television in the late 1990s, a televangelist called Amr Khaled took to the airwaves to preach that Islam did not conflict with "modern" ways. But he, too, made veiling his main message to women. A woman I know who was a regular follower of his shows told me she began to wear the hijab after listening to him talk so movingly about the importance of veiling. "I was in tears. I ran to my mother's closet and took out a head-scarf and decided to start veiling," she said.

Some of Egypt's neighbors, under similar influences, wrote the hijab into law at this time. In Sudan, under Article 152, enacted in the country's criminal code in 1991, the state imposes flogging sentences of up to forty lashes on women charged with violating the "Immoral Dress Provisions."

> Whoever commits, in a public place, an act, or con-
> ducts himself in an indecent manner, or a manner
> contrary to public morality, or wears an indecent,
> or immoral dress, which causes annoyance to public
> feelings, shall be punished, with whipping, not ex-
> ceeding forty lashes, or with fine, or with both.

Such language allows Sudan's "morality police" to pun-ish women for going unveiled or even for wearing trou-sers. Yet misogyny reflects hierarchy: Sudanese women who are arrested for "indecent dress" but who are from affluent or connected families can often get out of the flogging punishment altogether, or pay a fine to escape the pain and humiliation. Less advantaged women, and Christian women from the south—what became South

Sudan—are often the most affected by the notorious Article 152.

In countries where Islamists have pushed for veiling, the types of veils they promote are new. Unlike traditional forms of dress, which often had a much looser, more flowing aspect, the veils that Islamists promote are worn tightly around the head, often accompanied, in more conservative circles, with buttoned-down coats and cloaks in black and dark blue. Conversely, as the veil has become more prominent, many younger women, in Egypt and especially in Western countries, subvert the new austerity with neon-colored headscarves and form-fitting clothes that defy the modesty that is supposed to underpin veiling.

In 2005, I was assigned to interview the Muslim Brotherhood's spiritual leader at the organization's headquarters in Cairo. Although the Brotherhood had been officially banned, it was "allowed" to contest parliamentary elections that year. Its literature, banners, and flyers were visible in many neighborhoods across Cairo. I had stopped wearing a headscarf in 1993, and I fully expected to be asked to cover up for this interview; whenever I'd interviewed any Brotherhood leaders in the past, I'd been handed a scarf before being allowed to enter the room where the interview was to take place.

I was dressed in a short-sleeve T-shirt and trousers. This time the person who ushered me in did not hand me a headscarf; I was pleasantly surprised. My first interview was with Mohamed Akef, then the Supreme Guide of the Muslim Brotherhood. I told him that I'd heard that the Muslim Brotherhood was sounding more pluralistic than usual and that I'd come to see if it really was embracing diversity of opinion.

He told me the Brotherhood embraced pluralism and inclusion. To illustrate his point, he mentioned that after the Muslim Brotherhood in Kuwait, along with the ultraconservative Salafis, opposed the emir's plans to give women the right to vote and run for office, he—Akef—had written to them to remind them Islam did not forbid women's political participation.

Pleased that he'd introduced women's issues so early in our conversation, I asked Akef if the Muslim Brotherhood, should it ever govern Egypt, would change anything in the Egyptian constitution to curb women's rights, such as making the veil mandatory.

He insisted once again that the Muslim Brotherhood believed in pluralism and inclusion, and told me this:

"And as proof, you are here interviewing me and you are naked," Akef said.

"I am not naked."

"Your hair is naked, your arms are naked; according to God's law you are naked."

"The verses in the Qur'an regarding women's dress have been interpreted differently," I said.

"Don't listen to those who try to say hijab is not mandatory. There are no different interpretations. There is just one interpretation and according to that interpretation, you are naked."

So much for pluralism.

I only had to leave the Muslim Brotherhood's headquarters and take a look around me to understand why Akef wouldn't have to change anything in the constitution to make veiling mandatory. The Muslim Brotherhood had already won that battle. The veil, be it the hijab or the niqab, is a white flag raised to signal our surrender to the Islamists and their conservatism. Almost a decade after that interview, with the majority of women in Egypt covered by one form of veil or another, it is clear the Islamists have achieved region-wide social control.

When I talk about the need for a social revolution in order for our political revolution to succeed, I have this Islamist victory over social mores—as well as the definition of modesty—in mind, not just the regime's oppression.

I have never before written at length about my experience of either wearing or giving up the headscarf. It's always been a difficult subject, and for many of the years following my decision to stop wearing a headscarf, I was so ashamed that I preferred not even to mention to new acquaintances that there was a time when I wore the hijab. I wore a headscarf for nine years. It took me eight years to take it off.

When I lived in Egypt as a young child, none of my female relatives wore any kind of veil, and the only headscarves I saw were the casual handkerchiefs worn by rural Egyptian women. During the 1970s and '80s, however, women began to cover up more and more—this is noticeable when I look through old family photos. Aunts who thirty or forty years ago were getting married or attending weddings in sleeveless and knee-length dresses—and often posing next to belly dancers clad in sparkly, jangly bras, bikini bottoms, and flimsy, see-through skirts—are in today's weddings almost uniformly veiled. The majority of their daughters, my cousins, are also in the hijab.

In 1980, I returned to Cairo—my family's first trip back to Cairo since we moved to London in 1975—to find that my mother's youngest sister had decided to wear an especially austere kind of veil that consists of a head-to-toe tentlike cloak. This aunt is only four years older than me; we'd been very close as young children and practically grew up together. When we now walked down the street side by side—I was thirteen; she was seventeen—strangers would stop in their tracks and hurl abuse for the way she was dressed. Egyptians are generous with social commentary—my hair was so short back then that one young man walking behind us told his friend, "That girl used to be a boy and they gave her a sex change." But my aunt was on the receiving end of even worse vitriol.

"What the hell are you doing?" "What is that tent you're wearing?" (Now in Cairo, thirty-four years later, such abuse is hurled at women like me, who don't veil.)

Saudi Arabia changed everything for me. It was soon after my family arrived in Jeddah, when I was fifteen years old, that I first wanted to wear a headscarf. Religion was everywhere. The Committee for the Promotion of Virtue and the Prevention of Vice—the official Kafkaesque title of the morality police, also called the Mutaween or the Haya'—badgered shopkeepers and shoppers alike to attend prayers, and chased after women, urging them to cover up. None of this, of course, protected my body from men's roving eyes and hands. I needed something to defend myself, and I thought the hijab would. When I told my parents of my decision, they said I was too young to start wearing the hijab and suggested I wait a year or so.

Less than a month after we arrived in Jeddah, we went on hajj, or pilgrimage, one of the five pillars of Islam. Up until then, Mecca—the birthplace of Islam and the site of the Ka'aba, the cubical structure toward which Muslims pray five times a day—was a place I'd seen only in pictures hanging on the living room walls of family and friends. This trip was the first time I'd worn any kind of veil outside prayer time. I looked like a nun dressed in my white pilgrimage clothes.

One of the first rituals of the pilgrimage is *tawwaf*: circling the Ka'aba in order to pay respect to this sacred place and signal your intention to perform the hajj. Watching from above the hundreds upon thousands of Muslim men and women circle the Ka'aba is like watching a turntable spin, smooth and breathtaking in its motion.

You're supposed to circle the Ka'ba seven times, and as I slowly walked around it, reciting prayers along with my family, in a moment of great significance and sanctity, I felt a hand on my ass. I had never before been touched on that part of my body (or anywhere else, for that matter) by a man. I could not run, and even if I had possessed the courage, I could not turn around to confront the man who was groping me because the space was so crowded.

I could not put into words what was happening to me. I could not understand how, at this holiest of holy places, the place we all turned to when we prayed, someone could think to stick his hand on my ass and to keep it there until I managed to squirm away. He was persistent. Whenever I broke free, he persisted in groping my ass.

I burst into tears, because that's all I could do. I did not have it in me to tell my parents the truth, so I told them the crowds were getting to me. We went up to an inner level of the Grand Mosque, one story up, to complete our *tawwaf*. Then we returned to the lower level and the Ka'aba once more to kiss the black stone, another ritual of the pilgrimage. Muslims are taught that the stone was once translucent and white but that, over time, it has lost the allure of paradise and become tainted with the sins of humanity.

My mother and I had to wait for the women's turn. A Saudi policeman who was standing there signaled to the men to wait while we kissed the stone. As I bent toward the stone, the same policeman surreptitiously groped my breast. Surreptitiously: I came to learn during my years in Saudi Arabia and then in Egypt that this was how most men did it. That's how they got at your body—so surreptitiously that you ended up questioning your own sense of having been violated; your disgust at what happened; whether, in fact, fingers actually did poke through the underside of your seat on a bus or ever so lightly brush against your ass as the man to which those fingers belonged looked the other way.

If a policeman standing next to the Ka'aba in Mecca gropes my breast, what chance do I stand of complaining and getting anything done about it? Silence and shame are quick and early lessons. If a policeman who tells the men to stand aside so that women can kiss the black stone unhindered gropes my breast there, right next to the holiest site for Muslims, what chance do I or other women stand of fighting violations of our bodies?

It took me years before I could talk about being groped during hajj. I kept silent not only out of shame but so that Muslims would not look bad. Even now, when I do talk of being groped during hajj, I get accused of making it up or told that I'm maligning Islam. Yet several women have told me of similar violations as they performed holy rituals. How less likely would such violations of our bodies be if all the energy that went into trying to shut us up went toward stopping the men who grope us!

One evening, back in Jeddah, we took a gypsy cab for our weekly grocery shopping. The young man who dropped us off at the Jeddah mall where we shopped insisted on waiting so he could take us back home.

"Uncle, I want to ask for your daughter's hand in marriage," the driver, who was in his twenties, told my dad, who sat next to him in the passenger seat on our ride home.

"But she's fifteen."

My mother, brother, and I were in the backseat trying very hard not to laugh.

"That's okay. I still want to marry her."

"In our family, no one gets married until they finish university, my son."

"That's okay. I'll wait for her."

We laughed a bit more when we got home, but the "she's fifteen" followed by "that's okay, I still want to marry her" was not the stuff of humor. Soon after, a much older man, who caught me browsing the notice board in a su-

permarket while my parents were paying for their pur-
chases, asked me if I was alone. After I told my parents
what had happened, I was not allowed to go anywhere
alone again. My brother had to be with me at all times—
an early lesson in restricting a woman's freedom of movement in the name of protection.

By the time we went for our second hajj, my mind
was ready to surrender and my body was desperate for
invisibility. It felt as if everything were *haram* (prohibited) in Saudi Arabia. I was descending into my first of
several depressions; I felt I was losing my mind. So I
struck a deal with God: They keep saying a good Muslim
woman covers her hair, so I'll cover my hair if you save
my mind. I decided to wear the veil, and this time my
parents accepted my decision.

But I found that the hijab did not make me invisible.
I had decided to hide my body the way teenage girls,
newly aware of male attention, sometimes take refuge in
baggy clothing. Still, the garments I wore did not protect
my body from wandering fingers and hands. If I were
to use paint to indicate the places where my body was
touched, groped, or grabbed without my consent, even
while wearing the hijab, my entire torso, back and front,
would be covered with color.

Although living in Saudi Arabia made me choose
the headscarf, I wore it less frequently there than you
might think. Covering up, the majority of scholars said,
was required only in the presence of men who were not

relatives (although such interpretation has been challenged, as I mention above), and gender segregation at my school meant that I spent most of my day in the company of other women and could remain unveiled. However, when I returned to London with my family for vacations, the need to wear the headscarf—at least under the rules and regulations I had submitted myself to—presented itself at all times. I wore my hijab almost all day, and began to feel suffocated by it. It pulled at my throat. I felt constricted and confined, and missed feeling the wind in my hair. When I look at photographs of myself from that time, I see a girl who is cut off from the world, as though her headscarf sealed in the sadness she felt.

Despite the sadness, I was doing well in school. If wearing the hijab was causing or exacerbating my depression, no one would have guessed it. I wrote an essay about the ubiquity of women's head coverings across different religious faiths, which argued that it was unfair to associate the veil exclusively with Islam. What about nuns, or ultra-Orthodox Jewish women? I asked. I was keen to defend my commitment to the headscarf, and to connect to other religions the notion of modesty to which I had submitted.

Then I discovered feminism.

At the age of nineteen, I stumbled upon those incendiary books at the university library in Saudi Arabia. What was most startling to me was to read arguments by Muslim women—such as Mernissi and Ahmed—questioning the headscarf. Why were women alone responsible for sheltering men from the sexual desires women supposedly elicited in men? Why could men not control themselves? Why, if men were the ones being tempted, were they not the ones being policed? All these questions pressed themselves on me at a time when I was trying to push them away. They were both welcome and unwelcome, a sign that a reckoning between me and my headscarf was inevitable.

My escape route was to emphasize the idea of "choice." If a woman had a right to wear a miniskirt, surely I had the right to choose my headscarf. My choice was a sign of my independence of mind. Surely, to choose to wear what I wanted was an assertion of my feminism. I was a feminist, wasn't I?

But I was to learn that choosing to wear the hijab is much easier than choosing to take it off. And that lesson was an important reminder of how truly "free" choice is.

When I returned to Egypt at age twenty-one, the hijab became a full-time job, the duties of which I had not anticipated. Back then, in 1988, before neon-pink and orange hijabs and skinny jeans, there were more fixed ideas about what a woman in a hijab could and could not do. The strange combination that I represented complicated that equation: an Egyptian woman with a very English accent and broken Arabic, who danced along to music on campus in her hijab. Back then, that was not a comfortable combination. But trying to persuade people that I could make it work became a bit of an obsession.

I'd ride the metro and think to myself, I can't let the team down. What will people think about Muslims if I take my headscarf off after all I've said and done to prove you can wear one and still be an extrovert and a feminist?

At that time I began meeting and interviewing Egyptian feminists, drawing sustenance from the real women who led the struggles I had read about. I looked for them everywhere I could. Many of the older women practically adopted me, inviting me to their meetings, sending me their latest reports, and alerting me of important conferences they were holding. One of those mentors, Hala Shukrallah, became the first woman to lead a political party in Egypt when the social-democratic Dostour Party elected her its head in 2014.

One day, I interviewed a veteran journalist who was doing exactly what I aspired to do: using her writing to fight for women's equality.

"Why are you covering your hair?" she asked me.

For Shukrallah and the other feminists from the New Woman Foundation, my hijab had not been an issue. So when this journalist brought up my headscarf, she blindsided me. I wasn't there to talk about myself, but I became Exhibit A as she explained the conservative forces at work against Egyptian women.

"Can't you see you're destroying everything we've worked so hard for?" she asked me.

At the time, I could not. I was such an enthusiastic self-identified feminist, and the thought that I was letting the sisters down horrified me.

"But I've *chosen* to dress like this," I replied.

That word choice again.

What finally helped me part ways with the hijab was an anecdote my mother relayed from a conversation about me she'd had with a physician who was a coworker of my father's. It helped put to rest my conflict over that word, *choice*. The physician, asking after my brother and me, wondered if I was married. When my mother told him I wasn't, he replied—as she conveyed to me—"Don't worry, she wears a headscarf. She'll find a husband."

Just like that, a piece of cloth had superseded me.

Then I understood—as this man's patronizing confidence in my scarf had shown—that I wasn't the Hijab Poster Girl I thought I was. I was just a hijab.

When I so quickly replied, "But I've *chosen* to dress like this," I had not considered men, such as that physician, for whom my choice was irrelevant (just as my choice was irrelevant to the journalist). I realized that the journalist and the physician were on opposite sides of a struggle, and I knew that I did not want to be on the physician's side.

The week I finally decided to stop wearing a headscarf,

I had just finished my graduate studies in journalism at the American University in Cairo. You could count on maybe two hands the number of women in headscarves at AUC during the time I studied there, from 1988 to 1992. In those years, I was in the headscarf-wearing minority off campus as well.

My two biggest challenges on the day I parted ways with my headscarf were, first, telling my family, who had pressured me to keep it on during those eight years of struggle; and second, getting a bad haircut. I did not want anyone to think I'd taken off my headscarf for vanity's sake or to attract men. My feminism at the time meant I did not wear any makeup, did not pluck my eyebrows, and rejected "femininity" with a passion (except for skirts and color-coordinated headscarves).

So the last thing I wanted was to "look good" after I took off my hijab, and the best way to guarantee that was to go to a female hairdresser. In Egypt, at least before the majority of women donned the hijab, hairdressing was considered a profession of ill repute for women, and was dominated by men. So I went to a local hairdresser and asked for a woman. They asked if I was sure, but I was adamant.

Wonky haircut secured, and wearing my headscarf just halfway up my head, I went to pick up my sister from school, where I knew my mother would join me. As we waited for the girls and boys to dash out, I told my mother nervously what I'd done.

Those final days of my struggle with the headscarf took place during a heat wave, and I used the weather as an excuse to hide at home for a few days, putting off the delivery of my news to friends and peers. I finally forced myself out of the house, convinced that everyone I passed on the street and on the transportation I took to get to AUC knew that my bare head was a new thing, that I had just that day finally stopped wearing a headscarf. It didn't get any better at AUC, where my friends were split between the "You look so much better!" camp and the "What have you done, you've made us look so bad!" camp. To a friend from the latter camp, I replied, "I'm not the Qur'an in motion." But it didn't do much good.

Guilt clung to me for several years. I assuaged it somewhat by continuing to wear my old hijab-appropriate clothes, minus the headscarf. I was so ashamed that I'd taken it off that I would never tell new acquaintances that I used to wear the hijab. I didn't wear makeup, my hair remained short, and I had to reckon with a new body consciousness. Wearing the hijab for nine years had allowed me to put off defining what femininity meant to me. The hijab had been my way of trying to hide from men, but in the end it had only hid my body from myself.

One morning in 2002, a click on a Human Rights Watch e-mail ignited all that I'd left unspoken and unchallenged, all that I had tried to forget.

The fire was a tragedy that could have struck anywhere. Fifteen girls between ages thirteen and seventeen were trampled to death, and fifty-two others were hurt, when a blaze swept through their school.

Parents and journalists angrily demanded the resignation of education officials they accused of incompetence and corruption. There was plenty to be angry about. Some 800 schoolgirls were crammed into a building designed for only 250. The main gate to the school was locked. There were no emergency exits, no fire alarms, and no fire extinguishers in the building. Yet a far more sinister detail in this particular tragedy shows that it could not have happened anywhere but in Saudi Arabia.

Firefighters told the Saudi press that morality police had forced the girls to stay inside the burning building because they were not wearing the headscarves and abayas that women must wear in public in that kingdom. One Saudi paper reported that the morality police had stopped men who tried to help the girls escape the building, including firefighters, saying, "It is sinful to approach them." Girls died because zealots at the gate would rather have seen them burn than appear in public dressed inappropriately.

You are your headscarf. Your headscarf is worth more than you.

I could not stop crying as I read through the HRW

report. Those girls could have been my younger sister, who was at a school in Jeddah at that time. Whose Islam is it that allows men to condemn little girls to death?

That school fire and the Saudi state's complicity in the deaths of those girls should have sparked protests—a revolution, even! Every year, their deaths should be commemorated and reflected upon as the fatal consequence of misogyny. Yes, misogyny can kill you. Those schoolgirls should forever be commemorated as victims of a hate crime—the crime of hating girls and women.

But they are not commemorated or honored, and the revolution in Saudi Arabia is still far off.

The closer you are to God, the less I see of you—so goes the thinking behind the niqab. I find this idea extremely dangerous. It comes from an ideology that wants to hide women. Many people say that they support a woman's right to choose to wear the niqab because it's her natural right. But what they're doing is supporting an ideology that does not believe in a woman's right to do anything *except* cover her face. In Saudi Arabia, for example, Salafi ideology ensures that women cannot travel alone, cannot drive, cannot even go into a hospital without a man's permission. Yet some claim that the right that Muslim women are fighting for is to wear the veil, to cover their faces. I'm outraged when people say that as a feminist I must support a woman's right to do this. To claim that the wearing of the niqab is a feminist issue is to turn feminism on its head.

What disturbs me about the discussion of veiling in Europe is that the headscarf and niqab bans there are driven almost solely by xenophobic right-wingers. They're hijacking an issue that they know is very emotional and very easy to sell to Europeans scared about immigration and the economy, Europeans who don't understand people who look and sound different from them. As a result, the bans fail to find support among those who see them as a form of Islamophobia rather than what they really are: a women's rights issue.

The racism and discrimination that Muslims face in many countries—such as France, which has the largest Muslim community in Europe—are very real. But we must not sacrifice women at the altar of political correctness, or in the name of fighting the powerful and growing right wing in countries where Muslims live as a minority. I'm disappointed with the left wing in Europe for not speaking up and declaring that the niqab ban has everything to do with women's rights; we are fighting against an ideology that does not believe in women's rights. This is why I support the bans on the face veil that have been imposed in France, Belgium, and some parts of Barcelona, Spain. It is why I question why so many

Muslim men jump to defend the niqab and the right to wear it.

Witness my own run-in with one such Muslim man, the well-known academic Tariq Ramadan, the Swiss-raised grandson of the founder of the Muslim Brotherhood, Hasan al-Banna. Ramadan has written extensively on being Muslim and Western, and has often been looked to as a positive influence helping young European Muslims navigate their multiple identities. I personally find several of his positions too conservative.

During an appearance on the BBC television program *Newsnight* in which we were asked to react to the French ban on the niqab, Ramadan went to great lengths to explain that he believed that the conversation about the niqab should remain within the Muslim community. I find that argument disingenuous. Although on the surface it sounds quite reasonable, women have little room to dissent within that community.

Perfectly on cue—I could not have orchestrated it better myself—when the *Newsnight* presenter Jeremy Paxman saw me shake my head in dissent to Ramadan's words and commented that I seemed to disagree, Ramadan would not let me have my turn to speak and interjected with the outrageous claim "Of course you disagree. We all know that you are a neocon."

He was referring to the neoconservatives of U.S. politics, whose positions I have never identified with.

He understood—especially because of neocon support for the U.S. invasion of Iraq, which I marched against when I lived in New York City—that by saying this, he was maligning me.

After Ramadan interrupted several of my attempts to explain why I disagreed with him that the conversation on the niqab must remain strictly within the community, I yelled at him to stop talking because it was my turn and went on to explain that his behavior perfectly exemplified the hazards of insisting the community alone take care of an issue: the men spoke for everyone.

It was, as a friend described it, as if he were saying "Shut up woman, and let me fight for your right." Since that run-in with Ramadan, the term *mansplaining* has become popular for describing a man's insistence on explaining a woman's experience to her.

Niqab bans continue to gain ground in the European Union. In July 2014 the European Court of Human Rights upheld France's 2010 law that says that, in a public space, nobody can wear clothing intended to conceal the face. The penalty for doing so can be a €150 fine (about $205). The court ruled that the ban "was not expressly based on the religious connotation of the clothing in question but solely on the fact that it concealed the face." This ruling is exactly how the issue should be considered: the effects of concealment must be considered before religious connotation.

Arguments against the niqab can be made on grounds

of security: for example, a person in a mask cannot enter a bank, and the niqab can be considered a type of mask. I prefer a more philosophical argument. We are social creatures, and nonverbal communication is an important part of our daily interactions. If I were sitting in front of you now, our interaction would be very different depending on whether you could see my face. When we leave our homes, we enter into a social contract with the community we live in. Face veils, I believe, violate that contract by diminishing the ability to interact fully because of the way they impede nonverbal communication.

Some have argued against a ban on the niqab by claiming that the state must not play a role in people's choice of wardrobe. I find this a disingenuous argument that ignores the fact that the state already does this by banning nudity in public, for example. The state of New York, where I lived for ten years before I moved back to Egypt to write this book, forbids the wearing of masks in gatherings of three people or more.

An interesting and necessary tension in the discussion over veiling has developed over the past decade with the growing visibility of Muslim communities in the "West." I spoke earlier of how in Egypt, for example, the push and pull on the hijab was often articulated as a tug-of-war between "Islam" and the "West." Well, then, what happens when you are a Muslim who lives in the West? What happens when you are both Islam and the West? These increasingly visible identities will, I hope, help push us out of the binaries of Islam versus the West.

Ironically, the bans on the niqab could force a much-needed argument over the face veil that too many Muslim communities are scared to have. We must take apart the idea that the niqab is the pinnacle of piety for women—I have heard some religious scholars even say that if a woman is "too beautiful," she is obliged to cover her face. We must examine how the niqab contributes to the promotion of a "purity culture"—to borrow a phrase that feminists in the United States have began to use against Christian conservatives there who obsess over women's "modesty"—and how such a culture directly contributes to the dangers girls and women face in public space. Also, we need to hear more Muslim women's voices. After I stated my support for niqab bans—and clearly condemned the racism and xenophobia of the political groups behind those bans—I heard privately from Muslim women who opposed face veils of all kinds but who were reluctant to speak out because of the avalanche of attacks I was subjected to after I so publicly supported the bans and opposed face veiling.

Often when I speak in various Western settings, such as on university campuses or on television shows with a studio audience, a Muslim woman will challenge me on my opposition to the niqab and my support for its ban. I relish the back-and-forth we end up having because it's an important reminder that Muslim women disagree—

we are not monolithic in our views. It's also a healthy lesson in challenging what we've been taught is accepted scholarly interpretation. When I was younger and I would hear from men and women around me that it was the responsibility of an especially beautiful woman to cover her face so that she would not tempt men (again, the idea that the onus is on women to save men from themselves), it made me very uncomfortable, but I was timid in struggling with my headscarf and didn't have the language or the ability to challenge the absurdity of such a line of thought.

An Egyptian American woman who wears the niqab was featured along with me on a public radio discussion about the face veil, as well as on a CNN segment that has since gone viral on YouTube. On the public radio show, she explained that she began to wear the niqab after she worked on an oil rig as a chemical engineer and had been subjected to sexual harassment by male colleagues. Again, that "choice" to hide behind a veil, as I had done in Saudi Arabia. But in her case it was the full veil, which covered her face, which I consider an erasure of her identity. Over and over, because of men's sexual transgressions—in her case, here in the United States— women conceal their bodies. When the presenter of the radio show asked her if the niqab had affected her work life at all, the woman confessed that it had made it difficult to continue as a chemical engineer and that she had resigned from her job. That is an important point to remember. When I make the argument that the niqab erases a woman by concealing her face, I am often met with howls of disagreement from those who claim that women who cover their faces are as active as anybody else. That is clearly false.

Another encounter I had with a woman who wears the niqab was during the filming of the Al Jazeera English television show *Head to Head*. Filmed at the Oxford Union, the show has a debate-style format in which host Mehdi Hasan grills the guest on the subject at hand—in my case, my essay "Why Do They Hate Us?" and gender equality in the Middle East and North Africa—after which a panel of experts and then the audience pose questions.

One woman in a niqab chided me for not allowing her to struggle with her niqab in the way I had with my hijab. By supporting a ban on the face veil, she claimed, I was preventing her from completing her own journey. I told her I respectfully disagreed with her and wished her the best but that I still supported a ban on the niqab.

At the postshow reception, where men and women mingled, the same woman approached me without her niqab. I was shocked and asked her to explain why she wasn't covering her face. She said that it was complicated and that she covered her face depending on the situation. I told her that women in the Middle East and North Africa did not have such a privilege.

I maintain that Muslim women who live in Western countries—and are themselves both Western and Muslim—can help lift us out of the Islam-versus-the-West dichotomy. But I implore them to recognize the privilege that allows them to make vocal and impassioned defenses of the hijab. It is easy to forget that there are women with less privilege than they who have no true choice in veiling. I understand the need to defend one's headscarf—I did it for years, even as I was privately struggling with it. It's an important defense in the face of Islamophobes and racists. I get that. But if it's done without cognizance of the lived realities of women who do not have the privilege of choice, then my interlocutors end up doing exactly what they accuse me of doing with my support of a niqab ban: silencing other women. Why the silence, as some of our women fade into black, either owing to identity politics or out of acquiescence to Salafism? The niqab represents a bizarre reverence for the disappearance of women. It puts on a pedestal a woman who covers her face, who erases herself, and it considers that erasure the pinnacle of piety. We cannot continue to don the black veil and raise a white flag to Islamist misogyny.

Egypt and Tunisia provide two interesting and opposite examples of the impact of the revolution on veiling, and give intriguing hints to which way the pendulum will ultimately swing.

I have heard from and read about several women in Egypt who stopped wearing the headscarf or the niqab after the revolution that began in January 2011. The feminist activist and blogger Fatma Emam wrote an impassioned blog post on how she decided to stop wearing the hijab because she concluded that in order to liberate Egypt, she first had to liberate herself. Emam told Bloomberg News that her mother accused her of wanting to be a man and threatened to disown her if she joined the protests in Tahrir Square. (Emam was twenty-eight years old at the time.) She went anyway.

"There are so many women who like me defied their families," Emam told Bloomberg. "The revolution is not only taking place in Tahrir, it is taking place in every Egyptian house. It is the revolution of fighting the patriarch."

Another Egyptian woman told me she had removed her hijab while chanting "Liberty" as she marched along with thousands of others in January 2011, because at that moment that was what liberty felt like for her.

Two women who belong to a support group for women that I started in Cairo soon after I moved back in 2013 stopped wearing the hijab after the revolution. One of them, a thirty-five-year-old, told me:

"I took off my headscarf and I began to demand rights. The revolution has made me much bolder. I'm now much more likely to speak and know I'm entitled to demand my rights, especially when it comes to men. It's my right to have men respect me as an equal and not as a follower. What the revolution changed was our mind-set; it empowered us to say, who am I, who am I in this country and when am I going to get my rights?"

Another woman in the support group made the decision to leave home—still a huge taboo in Egypt—at the age of nineteen because her mother threatened to lock her up at her home if she removed her hijab.

It remains to be seen if these women, emboldened to unveil, will inspire more women. I hope so. I still get e-mails and messages on social media from women distressed by their struggles with their families over their hijabs. One woman I know removed temporarily her headscarf at a doctor's suggestion to treat a scalp infection. Her outraged mother contacted a cleric and asked him if she should disown her daughter.

In Tunisia under dictator Zine al-Abidine Ben Ali, women were prohibited from veiling in state-owned schools and institutions. Fatoum Alaswad, from the Ennahda Party, told me that during her law school days she would wear a beret so that she could observe hijab but still attend university. But after Ben Ali fled Tunisia the pressure against veiling reversed. Reports began to surface that Salafists were pressuring and at times attacking women who didn't wear the hijab. Tunisian feminist activists such as Amira Yahyaoui, who founded Al Bawsala (a first-of-its-kind watchdog in the region that monitored the writing of the constitution and threatened to name and shame constituent assembly members who tried to derail the clause on equality between men and women), explain that even though Tunisia might be more progressive than neighboring countries, it is conservative and patriarchal, especially in the smaller towns and rural areas.

Yahyaoui told me (for my BBC World Service radio documentary *Women of the Arab Spring*) that when she first asked a Salafist member of the constituent assembly a question, he refused to answer because, he said, he did not speak to women who were "naked." I laughed and told her the supreme guide of the Muslim Brotherhood also had called me naked. Enraged at the Salafist's description and the way he ignored her, Yahyaoui began to undress. Horrified, he asked her what she was doing.

"I'm showing you what a naked woman looks like," Yahyaoui answered. The man pleaded with her to stop and took her question. She told me that when the constitution passed, she looked for the Salafist and hugged him in celebration.

I met Lina Ben Mhenni, a linguistics teacher at the University of Tunis and a blogger who was active in the revolution, at a coffee shop from which she could see the Interior Ministry, where her father was tortured under the Ben Ali regime. For the previous six months, Ben Mhenni, thirty, had been under round-the-clock police protection because her name was found on an assassination list of a well-known Islamist group. They targeted her because she defends women's rights, is secular, and doesn't believe in mixing politics and religion.

I asked Ben Mhenni how she felt about the lifting of the ban on veiling in state schools and institutions and about the increase in veiling that followed.

"I consider this as personal freedom," she said. "I know under the regime many women used to be arrested and even some beaten by police just because they were wearing a veil. I have an aunt who wears the hijab and she had been arrested several times. She's not extremist, and she's wearing it just because she wants to wear it. It's personal freedom but those people don't have to interfere with my freedom."

How has it impacted women's lives?

"One of my female students said her roommates were trying to force her to wear the niqab. She was wearing black clothes and the veil, almost the burqa. She said, 'I didn't used to wear this thing and now they forced me to do this.'"

In Ettadmun—one of the largest working-class neighborhoods in all of Africa—I met Fatma Jgham, a university professor and women's rights activist who established Tahadi (Challenge), an arts center that teaches young men and women graffiti, rap, and dance in order to advance their activism. She told me she had been threatened by some of the Salafist students on campus because she does not wear the hijab.

Asked about the article in the new constitution that

guarantees equality, she said: "Equality is a practice, it's not just about words, about having a nice clause in a constitution. Women are fighting many different types of extremism: economic extremism, cultural extremism, and various forms of violence. The real difference will come when I feel safe everywhere I go. If I stand here in the street, do you really respect me as a woman, can you guarantee my safety?"

One of the young women who attended Tahadi was a nineteen-year-old who wore a headscarf and whose mother, a hairdresser, did not. They were both happy that a clause on equality existed, but were more concerned with issues closer to home.

"The one thing I would change is the mentality, because people in the neighborhood all the time say, 'How could you let your daughter go to [Tahadi]? It's full of boys.' And I say, 'It's none of your business, this is my daughter, she likes to go here, so I let her,'" the mother said.

"I'm worried about the fundamentalist and extremist groups and especially concerned when I come home late from work. Sometimes I'll leave deliberately early so I won't run into them. We know our religion and I understand that wearing hijab is a personal choice. Sometimes I have clients who come to the salon wearing hijab and take it off inside because they're worried about men outside who are Salafi or from other fundamentalist groups who will look at them badly or force them to wear it."

In modern Tunisia, and throughout the region, wearing the hijab does not remain a real choice for women, and it cannot so long as this pervasive discrimination and violence flourishes. Almost a century after Huda Shaarawi removed her face veil, we are floundering—and we will continue to flounder as long as a woman's body remains the canvas upon which we signal our acquiescence to conservatism and patriarchy.

ONE HAND AGAINST WOMEN

For those of us
who were imprinted with fear
like a faint line in the center of our foreheads
learning to be afraid with our mother's milk
for by this weapon
this illusion of some safety to be found
the heavy-footed hoped to silence us
For all of us
this instant and this triumph
We were never meant to survive.

—FROM "A LITANY FOR SURVIVAL," BY AUDRE LORDE,

FROM *THE BLACK UNICORN*

Almost 100 percent of Egyptian girls and women report being sexually harassed. A 2013 United Nations report cites the actual figure at 99.3 percent, but my friends joke that the remaining 0.7 percent had their phones turned off when researchers tried to contact them. Before leaving her home, every woman I know braces herself for the obstacle course of offensive words, groping hands, and worse that awaits her in the streets she takes to school, university, and work. The same UN study also reported that about 96.5 percent of Egyptian women have experienced unwelcome physical contact, while 95.5 percent have been subjected to verbal harassment on the streets.

In Yemen, the activist Amal Basha published a study asserting that 90 percent of Yemeni women have experienced harassment, specifically pinching. "The religious leaders are always blaming the women, making them live in a constant state of fear because out there, someone is following them," Basha told the Associated Press. If a harassment case is reported in Yemen, Basha added, traditional leaders interfere to cover it up, remove the evidence, or terrorize the victim.

It is worth noting that nearly all women in Yemen are covered from head to toe. I would never connect a woman's outfit with any unwanted physical contact or verbal abuse, but our conservative societies do. The extraordinarily high incidence of harassment in Yemen gives the lie to the conservatives who claim women bring harassment on themselves by dressing "immodestly."

In Tunisia, largely considered more socially progressive than other countries in the region, laws do little to curb harassment, and the same cultural forces perpetuate it: a taboo against speaking out, an obsession with virginity, and victim blaming. Though Tunisia enacted a 2004 law against sexual harassment, activists complain that it places the onus on women to prove that the harassment occurs on a regular basis. The law is also tainted with moralizing language that claims to discourage the "infringement of good mores and sexual harassment."

In Algeria, when the first workplace sexual harassment conviction was handed down, in 2012, the verdict was celebrated as an important message to Algerian women that they could seek justice. Yet the guilty party, a television executive in his seventies, was penalized with only a six-month suspended jail sentence and a 200,000 dinar fine—the equivalent of less than $3,000.

These violations continue unchecked and unabated as our governments fail again and again to make serious efforts to protect girls and women in public space. Effective laws are not the only solution, but they would at least indicate a willingness on the part of government to take seriously any sexual violations against women. In countries where there are no statutes against street sexual harassment, let alone a proper definition of it that could help women who wanted to use the law against their harassers, women are further silenced through shame and taboo.

Witness what happened when Rula Qawas, the dean of the School of Languages at the University of Jordan, assisted and advised a group of her students in her feminist theory course to make a short film about the sexual harassment experienced on the university's campus. The film showed female students holding up signs that quoted the verbal abuse they'd heard. After the film was posted on YouTube in June 2012, it sparked both controversy and condemnation, not against the men on campus whose sexual harassment had been exposed, but at the female students, whose film was accused of making the university look bad.

The university president fired Qawas, to the anger of activists and academics alike. One group of academics, the Middle East Studies Association, condemned Qawas's arbitrary dismissal and urged the university president to end the "systematic and unpunished sexual harassment of female students on the university campus."

Street sexual harassment is not exclusive to the Middle East and North Africa. It is a disturbing reality for too many women around the world. But a combination of societal, religious, and political factors has made the region's public space uniquely dangerous for women.

Activists at the first-ever regional conference on sexual harassment, which took place in Cairo in 2009 and was attended by representatives from seventeen Arab countries, concluded that harassment was unchecked across the region because laws don't punish it, women don't report it, and the authorities ignore it. Sexual harassment of girls and women at work, in schools, and on the streets was driving them to cover up and confine themselves to their homes, said the activists.

According to the Associated Press, participants at the Cairo conference said men are threatened by an increasingly active female labor force, with conservatives laying the blame for harassment on women's dress and behavior. Activists said that some women had told them they had either taken on the face veil to try to escape the constant harassment or were considering dropping out of school or work altogether.

Levels of street sexual harassment have soared throughout the Arab world, and everyone asks why. One answer—always met with howls of denial from conservatives—is that the more women cover up, the more it lets men off the hook. The "purity culture" that exists across the Middle East and North Africa burdens girls and women with the responsibility for their own safety from sexual violence, and for ensuring they don't "tempt" boys and men. "Purity culture" is a term I first came across in the United States, where it is used to describe the religious right's rhetoric that stresses virginity and modesty as the way for women to attain "purity." I find it very appropriate as a way to describe the pressures women in the Middle East and North Africa are subjected to, and it reminds us how much the global religious right wing has in common.

Nesma el-Khattab, twenty-four, a lawyer at Cairo's Shehab Center, which advocates for girls and women, told me of the hurdles girls and women face in fighting back against street sexual harassment: "Their mother tells them cover up so you don't face harassment. The grandma tells them you're a girl, don't fight back, just shut up and take it. Their father tells them don't speak out against harassment because those boys you spoke out against will go and beat up your brother."

Remember the conversation I had with the woman in the niqab on the Cairo metro? Take that kind of thinking to an absurd and dangerous extreme and you end up with the leaflets that the feminist activist Shahrazad Magrabi found being distributed outside girls' schools in the Libyan cities of Tripoli and Benghazi in 2014. She spoke to me for the BBC World Service documentary.

They begin with two bizarre monologues juxtaposed. First, a rose describes how it is easily found on every street corner, it is cheap to buy, etc. Next, a pearl talks about how special it is because it is nestled within a shell and deep under the ocean so no one can see it. In other words, the rose is not special because everyone can see it and has access to it, while the pearl is precious because it is hidden away.

"They're doing great harm, they're using Islam as a weapon, as a tool. They say if you're a woman and you go out you're going to hell," Magrabi said.

"What I'm worried about is the way they're feeding the people that it's haram [a sin]; you see girls six years old wearing headscarves; you go to school and if a teacher has [boy pupils over the age of six], the teacher must cover her face to teach. I am Libyan. I was born here. I never left. What the hell are they talking about?"

This purity culture leads both men and women to unjustly blame women for the harassment they suffer. Women are criticized, and they criticize and police one another, for wearing clothes that are too tight, or the wrong color, the wrong length, the wrong style—it's always the woman's fault. Anything a woman does to alter her own appearance is taken as an incentive to abuse. According to a survey conducted by the Riyadh-based King Abdul Aziz Center for National Dialogue, 86.5 percent of Saudi men blame "women's excessive makeup" for the rising cases involving molestation. In a survey carried out in 2008 by the women's rights activist Nehad Abo El Komsan's Egyptian Center for Women's Rights (ECWR), the majority of two thousand Egyptian men and women blamed women for bringing street sexual harassment upon themselves, saying that harassment resulted because of how the women were dressed. The ECWR also reported that 62 percent of Egyptian men admitted to harassing women. Perhaps saddest of all the center's findings: unlike foreign women, most Egyptian women agreed that women should keep harassment to themselves, to avoid ruining their reputations.

To insist on "modesty" as a prerequisite for safety on the street is victim blaming with disregard for the facts of street sexual harassment. It also endangers the lives of women who do not dress as "modestly" as society determines they should. In the hope that men won't hiss obscenities at us and that their hands respect the boundaries of our bodies, we plead, "What if I were your wife, sister, or daughter?" Always the focus is on the woman, the object of the obscenities and assaults. Does she not deserve safe passage in public space unless she is identified by her relationship to a man?

We should instead be exposing and shaming the boys and men who would deny us that safety, and we should ask, "What if he were your husband, brother, or son?" The people who make our lives hell on the streets are men we know, men we are related to, and they should be the object of scrutiny instead of us.

Soon after the ECWR's 2008 survey was published, I wrote an op-ed for a privately owned Egyptian Arabic-language daily newspaper called *Al-Masry Al-Youm*, in which I noted some of the several times I'd been groped, been followed by strangers in their cars, and had a stranger expose his genitals in my presence. The newspaper's online comments section was filled with remarks by men who alternately asked, "Who do you think you are? Who would want to grope you?" (as if being sexually assaulted were a compliment) and "Of course you get groped, what did you expect? You took your hijab off!" In response to my writing that I was just four years old when a man first exposed his genitals to me—he had parked his car on our street in Cairo, pulled out his penis in front of me and a friend, who also was a toddler, and beckoned for us to come down from the balcony on which we were standing—one reader actually took the time to find my e-mail address so that he could write to ask me, "What was so special about you as a four-year-old that anyone would want to flash you?"

I was stunned at the male rage that flooded the comments. Surely the rage should be ours, should belong to women? The few women who did respond left comments chiding those men who couldn't believe how widespread street sexual harassment in Egypt had become.

"Ask your wife, ask your sister, ask your mother!" the women said.

One or two women told the enraged men something I hope terrified them: "Every morning before I leave the house, I keep my headscarf in place with pins. Those pins become my weapons against your hands on transport and on the street."

Then there are the states that assault women directly. Such state-sanctioned, or -directed, assaults—and this leads to the nature of the misogyny that is so prevalent in our region—treat the bodies of girls and women as state property, to be sexually violated as punishment for political dissent or the dissent of one's family members. State-sanctioned sexual assault is at times paradoxically a punishment for a perceived crossing of a societal sexual red line. It is almost as if the state wants to say, *You cannot use your body sexually, but we can.*

According to Human Rights Watch's 2014 World

Report, thousands of Iraqi women have been unjustly detained by authorities and have suffered beatings and sexual assault, all so that government forces can gain leverage against the women's male relatives suspected of terrorism or other crimes. Even as HRW brought this atrocity to the world's attention, Iraq's own Ministry for Human Rights dismissed the report, stating through a spokesperson that it was "exaggerated," and claiming that those responsible for the claims in it had already been identified by Iraqi investigators and would be held accountable. Yet as HRW points out in the introduction to that study on the abuse of women by the Iraqi justice system, this is slim comfort to the victimized women. "Both men and women suffer from the severe flaws of the criminal justice system. But women suffer a double burden due to their second-class status in Iraqi society."

Libya, during both the forty-two-year dictatorship of Muammar al-Qaddafi and the revolution that overthrew him, provides painful examples as well. In her book *Gaddafi's Harem*, Annick Cojean, a reporter for France's *Le Monde* newspaper, recounts how Qaddafi abducted young women, kept them as sex slaves, and forced them to take drugs.

As in all countries in the region, speaking about rape in Libya is a taboo that few are willing to break. Two of the women who spoke to Cojean, however, illustrate my point about state-sanctioned sexual violation as a form of multiple levels of punishment. "Soraya," who was twenty-two when Cojean spoke to her, said she was just fifteen when Qaddafi ordered that she be taken from her family and brought to live as a sexual slave whom he kept in a basement of his residence near Tripoli, Bab al-Azizia. Soraya's story was verified by the experience of another of Qaddafi's sex slaves, "Khadija," who belonged to the infamous coterie of female bodyguards with whom he traveled. Her story dismantles the myth that many media outlets painted at the behest of Qaddafi that those female bodyguards were some kind of Amazonian warrior feminists. According to Cojean's book, Khadija, kept by Qaddafi in the same basement as Soraya, was used to seduce dignitaries for future blackmail. Another woman, "Houda," who was also a schoolgirl when she was first raped by Qaddafi, was told that her compliance would free her imprisoned brother.

During the revolution to unseat Qaddafi, the International Criminal Court said it had collected evidence that he had ordered rapes as a weapon against rebel forces. The first woman to speak out was Iman al-Obeidi, who burst into a Tripoli hotel to tell foreign journalists how she was gang-raped by Qaddafi's troops. Reuters news agency reported on three other women who suffered a similar fate, and who had been targeted for the "crime" of criticizing Qaddafi in a video clip broadcast on an international television channel. Two of the women were unmarried, and Reuters reported they were never seen again. The third, known as "the Revolutionary," spoke at a conference in the capital, Tripoli, behind a face veil, to guarantee her anonymity. Married and pregnant at the time of her abduction by Qaddafi guards, she said she miscarried after she was raped in prison. "The Revolutionary" was in her twenties, and told the conference that her youngest fellow captive was fourteen and the oldest was her mother's age.

In February 2014, the Libyan cabinet, in an unprecedented move, decreed that women who had been raped during the uprising that toppled Qaddafi should be recognized as war victims. That decree, which needed congressional approval, would have put the women on the same level as wounded ex-fighters and would have entitled them to compensation. As 2014 progressed, however, Libyan politics disintegrated amid militia fighting, and it is unclear when and if such a decree will help survivors of the sexual violence that took place during the revolution.

The cabinet's acknowledgment came thanks to the incredible courage of the few women who spoke out knowing they could be shunned or killed by their families for revealing they had been raped. These women were supported by activists who have worked tirelessly to mitigate the government's neglect of these women and the wrath of their male relatives, activists such as Souad Wheidi, who according to Reuters created an archive of the sex crimes committed during the revolution. Before Wheidi's work, these rapes went undocumented:

Amnesty International told Reuters that it had not documented a single case of rape during the eight-month-
long civil war that ended Qaddafi's rule because the
victims would not speak out. "We think [multiple rapes]
might have happened but do not have any evidence," said
Amnesty International. "Everyone said, this happened,
but not in our town. It was in the town next door."

In addition to retaliation from government forces,
militias, neighbors, and their own families, rape survivors in Libya who report the crimes leave themselves
open to criminal prosecution under *zina*, the area of Islamic law governing unlawful sexual intercourse. The
Arabic word *zina* means "fornication" or "adultery," depending on whether the "sexual crime" was committed
by an unmarried or married person. Under most interpretations of *zina*, any extramarital or premarital sex is
criminal, and even rape victims are prosecuted unless
they can prove to the court's satisfaction that the alleged
intercourse was not consensual. That is a risk that women
in most countries across the region, not just Libya, face.

The well-armed and increasingly powerful militias
that have paralyzed Libyan politics since the end of the
Qaddafi regime pose their own lethal danger to Libyan
women. In March 2014, I interviewed Libyan activist
Zahra Langhli in Cairo for the radio documentary I
made for the BBC World Service on women's roles in the
revolutions. Langhli, a cofounder of the NGO Libyan
Women's Platform for Peace, lamented that Libya had

turned into a security vacuum that threatened women's physical and political existence. In such a vacuum, women's rights were not considered a priority, especially with so many detentions and reports of torture. According to Langhli, Libyan women were not just casual victims of violence; they were also being deliberately excluded from the political process. Despite winning 16.5 percent of seats in the 2012 elections for the General National Congress, female parliamentarians were not safe, Langhli said.

"Women have been on television and exposing the kinds of threats they've been receiving from their colleagues [in the General National Congress] either affiliated to militias or themselves militias," she said. "In Arab or Muslim countries the issues of honor and shame are important. We see many female activists, the kind of war they face every day, it starts with rumors and might end up with kidnapping, rape, or anything like that, but it's targeted against female activists and politicians.

"I think it's targeted and systematic against women activists specifically to shrink them out of political space."

Three months after I interviewed Langhli, prominent Libyan human rights activist Salwa Bugaighis was assassinated in her home in Benghazi, just hours after casting her vote in elections for a new congress. Bugaighis was a lawyer and a strong advocate of women's rights who took part in some of the earliest protests of the Libyan Revolution in February 2011.

She was also an outspoken critic of the militias, and

her killing was part of a string of attacks against politicians, activists, and journalists who'd spoken out against the armed groups that control much of Libya.

Less than a month after Bugaighis was murdered, a female lawmaker was killed in the restive eastern city of Derna, which is known as a stronghold of Islamic extremists. A Libyan security official was quoted by the Associated Press as saying that unknown assailants sprayed bullets at Fareha al-Barqawi near a gas station. She was a member of a liberal-leaning political bloc in Libya's outgoing parliament. Her husband was a longtime political prisoner under Qaddafi, the AP said.

Women in Syria—where an uprising against the regime of Bashar al-Assad that began in March 2011 has led to a civil war—have also been targeted with sexual violence and abuse both by regime forces and by armed groups. According to the Euro-Mediterranean Human Rights Network (EMHRN), between March 2011 and July 2013 some six thousand Syrian women were raped. A report issued by the group described how women were being targeted by snipers and used as human shields, often along with their children. Furthermore, the EMHRN said women were being either kidnapped so that they could be exchanged for prisoners or gang-raped in retaliation for their male relatives' actions.

"The stigma makes them socially unacceptable so they have to flee the area; some don't even have a chance to flee with their family members. They're very much left alone and isolated," the EMHRN spokesperson Hayet Zeghiche told the BBC.

Like women in Libya, Syrian women took part in their country's revolution, protesting alongside men and risking imprisonment, torture, and death. And as in Libya, sexual violence became a weapon of war to punish them and terrorize others.

Female Syrian refugees have also been subjected to sexual violence in camps outside the country. In December 2012, the International Federation for Human Rights (FIDH), in collaboration with the Arab Women Organization (AWO), sent an international fact-finding mission to meet with Syrian women who had fled to Jordan. The FIDH said its delegation visited three refugee camps (al-Zaatari, King Abdullah Park, and Cyber City), and held meetings with eighty refugees living outside "official" camps in Amman, Rusaifa, Dhleil, and Sama Sarhan (Zarqa Governorate).

The FIDH's report, "Violence Against Women in Syria: Breaking the Silence," states:

> It remains extremely difficult to measure the extent of crimes of sexual violence or to draw conclusions on patterns, in particular due to the stigma surrounding such crimes. However, all those interviewed reported having witnessed or heard about cases of sexual violence and said that the fear of being raped had motivated their decision to flee the country. Several of the

women interviewed gave indirect accounts of rape and other forms of sexual violence committed by pro-government forces during house searches, following arrest at checkpoints and in detention. There were also accounts of such crimes having been committed by anti-government armed groups.

Many of those interviewed also spoke of the risk of women being abducted, by all parties to the conflict, in order to obtain information or as bargaining tools for the release of prisoners. According to several women and organisations providing support services, survivors of rape are sometimes forced into marriage, in order to "save family honour."

Girls and women were not always safe in refugee camps. In October 2014 *The Christian Science Monitor* reported that "in the refugee camps and crowded Turkish towns on the border with Syria, impoverished Syrian women and girls are falling prey to criminal rings that are forcing them into sexually exploitative situations ranging from illicit marriages to outright prostitution." Several other media outlets have documented similar horrors in the camps in Jordan.

It is not just in countries with a security vacuum or those ripped apart by civil war that the state violates women's bodies. In April 2014 the website Morocco World News lamented that "in modern Algeria, in the twenty first century, a girl walking in the street, which is a male space par excellence in Arab societies in general, can likely be arrested by the police to find herself in a hospital for [a] virginity test." It went on to quote an Algerian news site that reported that two young women were subjected to virginity tests after they were arrested by police while on their way home from a birthday party.

"A gynecologist in a hospital in eastern Algiers admits that 'the cases of virginity examinations requested by the police are increasing,'" Morocco World News said. "These girls 'were terrified, shocked to have been arrested by the police to pass this kind of test,' the gynecologist adds. These tests are usually made [in] the presence of the mother in cases of rape, but to break into a girl's privacy and subject her to [a] virginity test can have the same traumatic effect of rape!"

Morocco World News also quoted a Facebook group called Algerie Fait, which claimed that three women in the city of Constantine, ages eighteen to twenty, had been subjected to virginity tests by the authorities after being questioned over their having a picnic. The website also quoted an unnamed lawyer who made it clear that these virginity tests were the authorities' way of punishing the young women for behavior it deemed unacceptable:

"This kind of test is an attack on individual liberty. What has virginity got to do with a crime or offense? Does it constitute an essential element of the offense?" the lawyer said. "There is no law that says a woman has no right to go out in the evening with a man."

A similar dynamic was in play when police arrested a fourteen-year-old in the conservative emirate of Ajman (part of the United Arab Emirates) in 2011 on an "adultery charge" after neighbors complained she was meeting a man on the roof of their building. The girl was detained in an adult prison for two weeks and forced to undergo a gynecological exam that determined she was still a virgin, the *Gulf News* reported. The man she was said to have been meeting (in his mid-twenties) was also arrested, but undoubtedly not subjected to a humiliating examination of his genitals.

In Egypt, we have reached the point at which the state can physically strip you of your veil, and forcibly examine your hymen, while claiming to protect you. During a 2005 protest, activists claim, our former dictator Hosni Mubarak's regime used plainclothes policemen and pro-regime thugs to sexually assault female journalists and activists. The protest was to call for a boycott of a referendum to allow multiple candidates to run in the presidential elections—up until then, Egyptians would vote yes or no for Mubarak. Activists did not trust Mubarak or his political system and felt that the referendum alone, without large-scale political reforms, would not guarantee free and fair elections. Male police officers, plainclothes security forces, and hired thugs contained female activists and journalists in a confined area, then groped and sexually assaulted those women caught inside the tight circle. At least one woman was pinned to the ground as several men pressed their bodies over hers, as if to mime the act of rape. Female activists and journalists had their headscarves, shirts, and skirts ripped off, and some were left almost naked, leading their male colleagues to screen them with their own bodies.

The next day, many of the activists who endured the assaults gathered for a protest to launch a short-lived movement called "The Street Is Ours." Some of the women held up their torn clothes from the day before. Some later tried to sue the regime. (Even though they had photographs and videos of the sexual assaults, the cases were dismissed for "lack of evidence.") Still other assaulted female activists spoke on satellite television about what had happened to them. This was one of the earliest attempts to throw off the gag of shame that prevents Egyptian women from speaking about sexual assault. Very few Egyptian women had ever previously made public their stories of survival. The impact of these testimonies was tremendous. It was the first time that many Egyptians had ever heard sexual assault openly discussed. I know that my own relatives were sickened and enraged when they heard the activists' testimony.

One young woman told me that hearing this testimony was the moment of her politicization: "Nothing is my decision and I have no power over anything: My parents decide what I study at university and whom I'll

in Cairo, and women resolutely stood their ground in Tahrir Square, refusing to leave despite Mubarak's snipers, police, and plainclothes thugs. Those first eighteen days offered a utopian vision of what Egypt could be.

Many female protesters spent the night outside, in the square, violating the family-imposed curfews that controlled their daily lives. Not everyone could overcome their family's rules, but for those who did, it was an unprecedented break with a code very few had challenged until then.

Many of my friends who spent nights out in the square told me they did not experience any kind of harassment, that men treated them with a respect and regard for their personal space and integrity that was unheard of on Egyptian streets before those eighteen days in Tahrir. One activist, however, told me he'd heard a few stories that challenged that idyllic image, but said that no one wanted to ruin the image of the revolution. I was not in Egypt during those eighteen days and cannot verify either case.

Whatever utopia existed in Tahrir, it was upended with a series of horrific sexual assaults that began on February 11, 2011, the day Mubarak was forced to step down and the day the South African television news correspondent Lara Logan, who reports for the U.S. network CBS, was sexually assaulted by a mob. Ever more audacious assaults followed, with impunity for the predators and bewilderingly little public outrage. On March 8, 2011, there was a small but determined protest demanding that Egyptian women have a voice in building the country's future—including the right to be president. Despite, or perhaps precisely because of, their active role in the revolution, the two hundred women who formed the protest (together with some male supporters) were optimistic. But they were met with opposition from men in Tahrir Square, according to *The Christian Science Monitor*, and were set upon by men from outside the square who yelled at and in some cases groped and sexually assaulted several of the women and a few of the male protesters.

"Go home, go wash clothes," yelled some of the men. "You are not married; go find a husband."

The next day, March 9, 2011, soldiers cleared Tahrir Square of those who had returned to protest the slow pace of change under the military junta that had taken over after Mubarak's ouster. The military arrested hundreds of demonstrators and threw them in military jails where many were tortured and beaten. According to human rights groups, seventeen female demonstrators were beaten, prodded with electric shock batons, subjected to strip searches, forced to submit to "virginity tests," and threatened with prostitution charges.

Less than a month after Mubarak had stepped down, the military junta that replaced him, ostensibly to "protect the revolution," had officers stick their fingers into the vaginal openings of female revolutionaries—women who should have been our heroes—ostensibly in search of a hymen, ostensibly to protect the military from accusations of rape by the detainees (because only virgins can be raped of course). In other words, the Egyptian military sexually assaulted Egyptian women so that they could not "falsely" accuse the officers of sexual assault. Samira Ibrahim, one of the women subjected to sexual assault, sued, but a military court exonerated a military doctor she had accused of conducting the tests, despite the admission by several members of the ruling military junta, the Supreme Council of the Armed Forces, that the tests took place. Ibrahim told an online newspaper: "The person that conducted the test was an officer, not a doctor. He had his hand stuck in me for about five minutes. He made me lose my virginity. Every time I think of this, I don't know what to tell you, I feel awful. I know that to violate a woman in that way is considered rape. I felt like I had been raped."

It should've been our moment of reckoning. It should have sparked another revolution. Yet nothing happened. In fact, Salwa el-Hosseiny, the first woman to reveal the "virginity tests," was called a liar and vilified for trying to turn people against the mantra "The army and the people are one hand," which was popular when the military seemed to be siding with the people in the final days of Mubarak's decline.

Perhaps "The army and the people are one hand" was

one of the most honest statements to come out of our revolution: one hand united and working against women, one hand that groped or beat women and tried to terrorize them out of public space, one hand that found it perfectly acceptable to force two fingers into a woman's vagina.

Those women had risked their lives to liberate Egypt, and yet their violation was met with silence. That silence points to a truth: the regime oppressed everybody, but society particularly oppresses women. The regime knows it can violate women because society subjects women to the same violations; it knows that society will not speak out for its own women. In return for unaccountability for its oppressions, the regime turns a blind eye to society's abuses, tacitly condoning harassment and assault.

Egypt's current president, el-Sisi, approved of the March 2011 "virginity tests." Since July 2013, when el-Sisi overthrew President Mohamed Morsi, who came from the Muslim Brotherhood movement, women who are affiliated with the Brotherhood—which has since been outlawed as a "terrorist group"—have also said they were subjected to "virginity tests" in detention. So it does not matter where you stand on Egypt's political spectrum: if you are a woman, your body is not safe.

In the years between Mubarak's downfall and the inauguration of el-Sisi, street sexual harassment, after being left unchecked for years, morphed into especially vicious mob sexual assaults against women at protests and public celebrations. Egyptian human rights groups documented 250 cases of mob attacks against women in Cairo's Tahrir Square and the vicinity between November 2012 and January 2014.

Egypt is an important case study in how state and street work in tandem to push women out of public space. It also demonstrates how regimes, regardless of ideology, have proven unwilling or fundamentally unable to address what Human Rights Watch has described as "an epidemic of sexual violence." One of the ways in which regimes and their supporters brushed aside and belittled concerns over women's bodily integrity was to blame their opponents for attacking women. As each group busily defended its men against such accusations, the women, who should have been their main concern, were left out of the conversation.

It took mob sexual assaults, including a gang rape in Tahrir Square during the inauguration of el-Sisi in June 2014, to finally force an Egyptian president to speak about sexual violence against women. El-Sisi paid a visit to the victim of that gang rape, who was recovering in a hospital, and apologized to her. He vowed to take "very decisive measures" to combat sexual violence and, addressing Egypt's judges, said, "Our honor is being violated on the streets, and that is not right." Yet it is women's bodies that are being violated, not Egypt's "honor."

Thanks to the tireless efforts of women's rights groups

and small but incredibly courageous initiatives launched to combat growing street sexual violence, including HarassMap, Tahrir Bodyguard, and I Saw Harassment, in 2014 the state finally acknowledged the problem and seemed to act on it, criminalizing the physical and verbal harassment of women and setting unprecedented penalties for such crimes. In July, five men were jailed for life for attacking and harassing women during celebrations of el-Sisi's inauguration in June. Reuters news agency reported that another defendant, age sixteen, was jailed for twenty years, and a nineteen-year-old was given two twenty-year jail terms, though it was not immediately clear if these would run concurrently or consecutively. All seven were convicted of sexual harassment, under the new law, and of attempted rape, attempted murder, and torture.

In a reminder of how our criminal justice system often raises more questions and dilemmas than it answers, one of the five men was sentenced to life on separate charges of attacking a woman as she celebrated the anniversary of the 2011 revolt that toppled autocratic president Hosni Mubarak. Are our police just rounding up the usual suspects?

El-Sisi's security forces must be held accountable for their assaults on female protesters. Until they are, their actions should be considered the height of hypocrisy. El-Sisi's interior minister has promised to create a new department to combat violence, including the sexual assault and harassment of women. But how will a police force that has harassed and assaulted women combat violence against women? How will that police force know how to act and what to do in cases of sexual assault and rape when it has no training in treating such crimes? Flourishes of words and chivalry are one thing. How those translate into concrete mechanisms that protect girls and women and ensure justice is another thing altogether.

In a dire irony, the extreme sexual violence has forced Egypt to pull ahead of other Arab nations in breaking the taboo of publicly discussing street assaults. Egypt's brave activists have begun the difficult and necessary task of deflecting the shame from our bodies onto those who insist on violating them.

Almost every part of my body has been groped or touched without my consent. These assaults happened in Saudi Arabia, where I lived as a teenager, and in Egypt, where I returned to live at the age of twenty-one.

The state first forced its hands on my body on Mohamed Mahmoud Street, where in November 2011 five days of clashes occurred between demonstrators trying to protect Tahrir Square and the soldiers and police who attacked the families of revolutionaries and burned the tents of peaceful protesters.

The details of what happened to me mattered little to

the triage nurse in the emergency room of the private hospital where, about sixteen hours after riot police had broken my arms and sexually assaulted me, I was trying to get medical care.

"How could you let them do that to you? Why didn't you resist?"

She might as well have asked me where my shame was. How could I "let" riot police sexually assault me, and how could I so brazenly describe what had happened to me? It had been many years since I was a virgin, but she was chiding me for my lack of moral virginity, if you will. A good virgin, a good moral virgin, would have "saved" herself from those men's hands; a good moral virgin would have saved her breasts and her genitals; a good moral virgin would not have been there on Mohamed Mahmoud Street in the first place. Finally, a good moral virgin would not have so openly described her sexual assault.

"When you're surrounded by four or five men from the riot police, and they're beating you with sticks this long, there isn't much 'resisting' you can do," I explained to the nurse.

I've spoken often about my sexual assault, usually with mechanical detachment. At first, I spoke in order to expose and shame not just the men who'd assaulted me but also the regime that had trained them to do so, that had set them as attack dogs on me and at least twelve other women on Mohamed Mahmoud Street. Divide and conquer takes on a new meaning when you tug on the jacket of the supervising officer who, as he witnesses his men groping every part of your body, assures you nonetheless that you are safe because he will protect you. Then, after he says he will protect you, in the very next breath he threatens you with gang rape by another group of his men, amassed close by and gesticulating at you.

Still, I needed a body, however imperfect and unreliable, between me and the men who were grabbing at me. I needed to believe that there was an authority figure who could protect me. I needed to pretend that the supervising officer meant what he said, even as his lie was demonstrated on my body. I have needed to say this over and over for my own reckoning with what I survived, and also because I came to learn that this pattern of assault—promises of protection as the assault is happening, alternating with threats of gang rape—was a modus operandi that had been used on other women during the battle with security forces on Mohamed Mahmoud Street.

Women have fought alongside men in political revolutions that have toppled dictators. But once these regimes fell, women have looked around to find the same oppression, sometimes inflicted by the men they stood shoulder to shoulder with, by men who claimed to be protecting them.

Listen to Donia and Mayada, two nineteen-year-old

women from a working-class Cairo neighborhood, whom I interviewed for my radio documentary.

"We had a revolution to improve our lives and things have gotten worse. It's dangerous to walk the streets. We don't feel safe at all, our lives haven't improved, and none of the things we wanted from the revolution have been achieved," Donia told me.

"Men around here look like at us like we're products in a shop. We have no rights. If you complain, no one listens to you and you could suffer the consequences of complaining. I want women to have a respected position and not be considered a product you can buy in a shop."

Said Mayada: "Our society by and large says your position as a woman in Eygpt is in your home, not outside. So women are not considered equal to men and a lot of men don't give you the respect you deserve. A lot of men don't make you feel like you belong outside with them, that your place is at home."

Just before I met Donia and Mayada, producer Gemma Newby and I had gone to a five-star hotel for an event called Egmadi ("toughen up"), in which women were taught the basics of self-defense and given a mood boost with dancing and Zumba exercises. The hall where the event was held was filled with mostly young women in their late teens and early twenties. Some older women had brought their daughters with them.

All the women I spoke to for the radio documentary

complained of constant verbal and physical sexual abuse on the streets and of an overall feeling that they were not safe in Cairo. Though there are many class disparities in Egypt and the rich are cushioned by several privileges, street sexual harassment spares no one, rich or poor. Once your feet are on the street, it matters little whether your can afford to attend an event at a five-star hotel or you live in a working-class neighborhood that does not have a police precinct. Being a woman anywhere is dangerous.

The regimes that governed the Arab world before the recent revolutions were united in an utter disregard for women's bodily integrity—a message that was not lost on the male public, who reflected back a similar disregard. Lack of accountability left both state and street misogyny to grow unchecked, producing the horrific incidents of sexual violence that recur day after day.

Unless we draw the connection between the misogyny of the state and of the street, and unless we emphasize the need for a social and sexual revolution, our political revolutions will fail. Just as important, women will never be free to live as autonomous citizens whose bodily integrity is safe inside and outside the home.

THE GOD OF VIRGINITY

Arab society still considers that the fine membrane which
covers the aperture of the external genital organs is the
most cherished and most important part of a girl's body,
and is much more valuable than one of her eyes, or an arm,
or a lower limb. An Arab family does not grieve as much at
the loss of a girl's eye as it does if she happens to lose her
virginity. In fact if the girl lost her life, it would be considered less of a catastrophe than if she lost her hymen.

— NAWAL EL SAADAWI, *THE HIDDEN FACE OF EVE*

Our hymens are not ours; they belong to our families.

This truth was brought home to me one evening
in Amsterdam, after I'd taken part in an event on the
rights of Muslim women. In a conversation that evening, probably the first conversation about sex I had
had with fellow Arab or Muslim women, a Dutch Moroccan woman told me and a group of her friends, "When I
first had sex, it was as if my mother, my father, my grand-
parents, the entire neighborhood, God, and all the angels
were there watching," We all convulsed with laughter.

It was a relief to talk to women who still understood the burden of virginity and the guilt involved in shedding it, women who did not judge. It was a relief to talk to women who would never ask, "How could you not resist?" as the nurse in the ER asked me when I told her I'd been sexually assaulted.

I actually "resisted" for a long time—too long, I believe when I look back now. I guarded my hymen like a good virgin until I was twenty-nine. I accepted and obeyed what I was taught by my family, who in turn were taught by their parents: no sex until marriage. Now, when I think about how long I waited to have sex, I am sad for my younger self and sad that I waited so long to experience and enjoy something that gives me so much pleasure. Back then, though, during all those years that I waited and waited, it would terrify me even to consider sex before marriage. I was taught by my family, by school, by religion, by society, and I obeyed. I'd been trained well and I was a "good girl" to the end. My hymen was protected from my feminism. My feminism wrestled with my headscarf but not with my hymen. Why?

Why did I obey? And why did I wait so long to finally disobey?

Those questions kept coming up again and again in, of all places, Oklahoma. There, in a University of Oklahoma lecture room where I was teaching a course on gender and new media in the Middle East, in 2010, I began publicly to share my reckoning with the god of virginity.

How do you discuss virginity with a class of American university students without the conversation sounding irrelevant to their lives or, worse, like an exercise in exoticizing another culture? Women, sex, and culture form a Bermuda Triangle in which open discussion tends to run off course, through either defensiveness (when students feel compelled to defend a cultural practice) or superiority (when they feel compelled to parade their culture as being above whatever cultural challenges are being discussed).

The personal is not only political; it demolishes this Bermuda Triangle. I received a powerful reminder about how much easier the personal makes it to discuss problems "over there" after I showed my class the Lebanese film *Caramel*, in which director Nadine Labaki plays the owner of a Beirut hair salon whose friends and coworkers portray a cross section of the Lebanese female experience.

One of the friends undergoes hymen reconstruction just before her wedding to a man she fears will reject her if he finds out she isn't a virgin. At first some students expressed shock that the woman could not share her sexual history with her future husband, while others wondered why it was such a big deal that she was no longer a virgin. I reminded the class that until the 1960s, virginity was a "big deal" in the United States, too.

"Have you heard of purity balls?" asked one young woman in the class, referring to formal dances in the United States between fathers and daughters at which teenage girls pledge to remain virgins until marriage. Such balls underpin purity culture in the United States.

Yes! I thought. Now virginity was "over here." I had indeed heard of purity balls, through news articles, but they seemed as foreign to me and to the class as hymen reconstruction.

Until the personal shook us out of our complacency.

"I just want everyone to know that I signed a purity pledge with my father," one of the students said.

I could not have engineered it better myself. Her courage in sharing reminded us all that virginity wasn't just far away in Lebanon or in newspaper feature stories. It was right in class with us. Oklahoma kept doing that to me. I joke that going there was like going to the Middle East: a similar mix of religion and conservative politics prevailed. Watching the way the U.S. religious right wing has managed to erode women's reproductive rights, especially in the South, I was struck by how important and courageous feminists and reproductive rights activists in those southern states are.

Some of the other students tiptoed around asking questions of the student who had shared her purity pledge experience.

"I respect that you think you've made a free choice," one student told her. "But [the American playwright]

Eve Ensler said that when you sign a pledge to your father, your sexuality is being taken away from you until
you sign it to your husband when you get married."

Teaching is like alchemy. You take a few students,
mix in some difficult subjects, and you are bound to be
stunned by the results.

I make my classes as personal as possible. I offer my
experiences to keep a face on the issue we're talking about,
so the least I could do to show my appreciation for the
generous sharing we had all witnessed—and to express
solidarity with a conservative position I once shared—
was to tell the class how long I had waited to have sex.
There were no purity pledges in my past, but there was
a time when I, too, believed I should wait till I got
married before I had sex—but then it took forever to
get married and I got fed up waiting.

When I was younger, I had no one to share this with.
My guilt was exacerbated by secrecy, and for a long time
I could talk about sex only with non-Muslim female
friends.

Now I've become bolder, yet it's not always recipro-
cated or appreciated. At one Muslim women's conference,
after I shared how difficult it had been to overcome the
guilt of premarital sex, another Muslim woman bluntly
told me that the Qur'an clearly stated that "fornicators
were for fornicators," so there was a "fornicator" out
there for me somewhere.

Charming.

Undeterred, and sometimes driven by an insatiable need to share—share and shed the guilt—I've found that my skin has thickened. I was made more resilient in Oklahoma. Some evenings, alone in my hotel room, weeping was the only way to let go of memories, some as old as twenty years.

Male-dominated religions and cultures, which cater to male sexuality with barely a nod to women's desires, are difficult enough to endure without the judgments of fellow women. I know where these judgments come from; I recognize the need to conform. That need internalizes misogyny and subjugation, so much so that mothers will deny daughters the same pleasure and desire they were denied, and will call them "whores" for seeking it. In order to survive, women police their daughters' bodies and their own, subsuming desire for the "honor" and the family's good name.

The god of virginity is popular in the Arab world. It doesn't matter if you're a person of faith or an atheist, Muslim or Christian—everybody worships the god of virginity. Everything possible is done to keep the hymen—that most fragile foundation upon which the god of virginity sits—intact. At the altar of the god of virginity, we sacrifice not only our girls' bodily integrity and right to pleasure but also their right to justice in the face of sexual violation. Sometimes we even sacrifice their lives: in the name of "honor," some families murder their daughters to keep the god of virginity appeased. When that happens, it leaves one vulnerable to the wonderful temptation of imagining a world where girls and women are more than hymens.

If they could, I'm sure many in our societies—families and clerics—would tie girls' legs together until their marriage nights. In some countries, communities do the next best thing and cut off perfectly healthy parts of girls' genitalia (the parts intended for pleasure), to curb sexuality until the girl and her intact hymen are handed over to a husband.

Female genital mutilation (FGM)—sometimes referred to as genital cutting and erroneously as "circumcision"— "comprises all procedures that involve partial or total removal of the external female genitalia, or other injury to the female genital organs for non-medical reasons," according to the World Health Organization (WHO). The main motivation behind FGM is to control female sexuality. It is believed to reduce a girl's sex drive, thereby helping to maintain her virginity and, later, her marital fidelity.

The procedure has no health benefits for girls and women. On the contrary, it can cause severe bleeding and problems urinating and, later, can produce cysts, infections, infertility, and complications in childbirth. FGM does not reduce sexual desire, but it does make victims less likely to experience arousal, lubrication, orgasm, and satisfaction during sex, according to a 2008 study conducted at the King Abdulaziz University Hospital in Jeddah.

According to UNICEF, more than 125 million girls and women alive today in the twenty-nine countries in Africa and the Middle East where FGM is concentrated have had their genitals cut. It is estimated that 30 million girls are at risk of undergoing FGM in the next decade. FGM is carried out mostly on young girls, sometime between infancy and age fifteen. After decades of misguided handwringing over "offending" a cultural practice—handwringing that paid little heed to a girl's bodily integrity—FGM is now designated a violation of the human rights of girls and women by a concert of international treaties, regional treaties, and political consensus charters.

In 1997 the United Nations and the WHO issued a joint statement declaring support for the abandonment of FGM. The next decade saw efforts to eradicate FGM in both law and practice by local agencies and international human rights organizations. Based on the lessons learned through these efforts, in December 2012 the UN General Assembly issued a stronger condemnation of FGM and urged its member nations to formally outlaw the practice. About half the nations that comprise the African Group followed this recommendation, though enforcement remains inconsistent throughout the cultures that practice FGM.

The WHO classifies FGM into four major types:

1. Clitoridectomy: partial or total removal of the clitoris (a small, sensitive and erectile part of the female genitals) and, in very rare cases, only the prepuce (the fold of skin surrounding the clitoris).
2. Excision: partial or total removal of the clitoris and the labia minora, with or without excision of the labia majora (the labia are "the lips" that surround the vagina).
3. Infibulation: narrowing of the vaginal opening through the creation of a covering seal. The seal is formed by cutting and repositioning the inner, or outer, labia, with or without removal of the clitoris.
4. Other: all other harmful procedures to the female genitalia for non-medical purposes, e.g. pricking, piercing, incising, scraping and cauterizing the genital area.

I must have been about eighteen or nineteen when I first heard about FGM, through a news magazine article that my friends and I found at the university library in Jeddah. We read the item on FGM in silence and terror. It was not something we (or at least I) associated with "us" at all. Soon after, though, I learned that many women in my extended family had been cut when they were girls, and I became obsessed with the thought that so many women I loved had been subjected to that cruel procedure. I needed to learn all that I could about this torture performed in the name of love and acceptance, and in denial of its searing physical, psychological, and emotional pain.

The cultural origins of FGM are obscure. In Sudan, infibulation (the most extreme form of FGM) is described as the "Pharaonic" method, and in Egypt the same procedure is known as the "Sudanese" method. This history matters little to the girls brutalized and butchered as their own mothers watch, and sometimes even help to hold them down. Can there be a greater betrayal? And in the name of love! Yes, love. These mothers do not hate their daughters. They have not forgotten the brutalization they themselves endured as their own mothers held them down. How could they? Surely they have not forgotten the pain. Yet they understand—as they hear their daughters' screams, echoes of their own screams of decades earlier—that without such butchery, their girls will be considered sexually out of control and unmarriageable. So they cut away to make them complete—the irony of cutting, of mutilating, to make whole!

The Egyptian feminist Nawal El Saadawi recalls her cutting at the age of six: "I did not know what they had cut off from my body, and I did not try to find out. I just wept, and called out to my mother for help. But the worst shock of all was when I looked around and found her standing by my side. Yes, it was her, I could not be mistaken, in flesh and blood, right in the midst of these strangers, talking to them and smiling at them, as though they had not participated in slaughtering her daughter just a few moments ago."

How does a girl survive this barbarism with her trust of other people intact, especially after her own mother was there and failed to protect her?

For the lucky few who escape, the god of virginity can creep up on you just when you thought you'd been safely delivered to a husband. In 1994, I covered the UN International Conference on Population and Development. One of the feminist groups participating gave me a report on reproductive rights in Egypt that it had prepared for the conference. Under the FGM section was a story that has never left me. A seventeen-year-old was returned to her mother's home on her wedding night with a note from the young woman's husband to his mother-in-law: "If you want your daughter to be married, you know what you need to do." On the spot, the mother called a traditional midwife to cut off the necessary flesh—a pound of flesh to mark the transaction, the handing over from home to husband, the transition from daughter to wife. Now do you understand why mothers will hold down their daughters and block out their screams? They know what must be done, what must be suffered, what must be silenced, and what must be said for their daughters to earn a husband.

The hymen contains no Off or On switch. A sex drive is not determined by the presence or absence of a hymen; nor is it determined by the clitoris or what remains of it after cutting. Where does desire really begin and end? That does not seem to be a concern to those who insist on FGM. The greater concern is that the family deliver a physical virgin to a husband who can then claim her hymen for himself. But virginity does not rest solely on that fragile membrane otherwise known as the hymen.

The Arab world raises its girls to remain forever mental and emotional virgins. How, after years of having it drilled into you that sex is dirty, that sex is a sin—when your genitals are cut and you are left to contend with the resulting physical and emotional trauma—are you suddenly to enjoy sex, let alone to express what you want?

There is a scene in the Egyptian writer Sonallah Ibrahim's novel *Zaat* in which the protagonist, the eponymous Zaat, a middle-class Egyptian woman, considers subjecting her daughters to genital cutting at her mother's insistence. Zaat discusses her misgivings with her best female friends, who dissuade her, reminding her of how their own cutting ruined their sex lives.

Why aren't more mothers coming to this conclusion? Why does it take a male writer to remind women that our society is denying us the right of pleasure? We must create our own ways of writing and speaking honestly about FGM, between women.

Early on during my research on FGM, what I can

only describe as destiny led me to Dr. Nahid Toubia. I was then an eager young feminist but I was unable to find the words to describe how heartsick I was that so many of the women I loved had been violated as girls through genital cutting. Dr. Nahid Toubia helped me find the words.

Toubia was the first woman to qualify as a surgeon in her native Sudan, and she has written extensively about FGM. She would tell me about her delicate discussions with her own mother about her mother's FGM, and when I asked her how I could be as delicate in my own conversations, she told me never to make the women we love feel like freaks for having been subjected to cutting.

A year or two after I met Toubia, Egypt was forced to confront FGM—not because the country finally understood that we were needlessly and heartlessly slicing our girls' genitals, but because CNN aired a video of a girl's cutting and her screams. That poor girl was violated twice—once by the hacking away at her flesh, and again by its airing on satellite television around the world. The video was broadcast right after an interview in which then-president Hosni Mubarak claimed that Egypt no longer practiced FGM. So it wasn't the horror of FGM that caused outrage, but rather that the president was made to look either mendacious or out of touch.

The local CNN producer—not the U.S. citizens who produced or reported on the piece—was arrested and charged, basically, with making Egypt look bad. And lo and behold, public service announcements followed in the ensuing years, billboards went up, and for about five minutes we paid attention to the pain of our girls—before sinking back into denial, leaving the heavy lifting to nongovernmental organizations whose tireless work over the years can only be described as Sisyphean.

That video exposed a horror that by 1994 had claimed at least 90 percent of ever-married Egyptian women between the ages of fifteen and forty-nine. When people in Egypt read those figures—issued by a multitude of organizations, ranging from UNICEF to the WHO, and most recently compiled in a 2013 UN study—they spend more time denying the veracity of the numbers than asking why we still subject our girls to FGM. In 2008 an Egyptian national health survey reported a drop in the prevalence of FGM, claiming that about 74 percent of girls ages fifteen to seventeen had undergone the procedure—giving hope that, despite all odds, those tireless NGOs were making some progress. But the genital mutilation of three-quarters of our girls is still horrific.

FGM is practiced by both Muslims and Christians in Egypt, where many believe it is a religious duty, despite the fact that it is not mentioned in either the Qur'an or the Bible. In 2008, doctors and nurses in Egypt were banned from performing genital cutting after a twelve-year-old girl died from an anesthetic overdose while undergoing the procedure at a private clinic in Minya, in southern Egypt. The ban imposes penalties ranging from three months to two years in prison and fines of up to 5,000 Egyptian pounds ($715).

But the ban on FGM has done little to curb the practice, which is still being carried out by traditional cutters and sometimes medical practitioners. While most deaths probably go unreported, every now and then a case makes it into the news, as when thirteen-year-old Soheir el-Batea died in June 2013 after a doctor at a private clinic in Daqahleya, northeast of Cairo, performed FGM on her at her family's request.

The medical report of her death described it as an allergic reaction to penicillin. The doctor who performed the cutting and Soheir's father stood trial in 2014, in the first case of its kind in Egypt. Finally, a chance for justice. The court acquitted both the doctor and the father. At the time of this writing, Human Rights Watch said it was unable to obtain the full final verdict explaining the acquittal. To coincide with the trial, the BBC produced a television segment in which the correspondent Orla Guerin found a traditional midwife who told her that despite the ban, she had a waiting list of mothers who wanted her to cut their daughters.

The *Guardian* newspaper found that many in Soheir's village of Diyarb Bektaris supported FGM and believed it was prescribed by Islam. Raslan Fadl, the physician who performed Soheir's cutting, was also a sheikh—an elder—at the local mosque, according to the paper.

"We circumcise all our children—they say it's good

for our girls," Naga Shawky, a forty-year-old housewife, told *The Guardian.* "The law won't stop anything—the villagers will carry on. Our grandfathers did it and so shall we."

A sixty-five-year-old farmer told *The Guardian* he did not realize that genital mutilation had been banned. "All the girls get circumcised. Is that not what's supposed to happen? . . . Our two daughters are circumcised. They're married and when they have daughters we will have them circumcised as well."

Calls to reverse the ban on FGM continue to issue from Islamists and some doctors who claim that girls are more likely to die if their families take them to traditional cutters. Those same doctors conveniently ignore the deaths that have already occurred in private clinics.

Hosna, a fifty-three-year-old widow and a survivor of FGM, told me when we met at the Shehab Center that she cared little for the ban.

"Cutting happens whether it's against the law or not; it must be carried out because that's the way to maintain the purity of girls to make sure that the girl is not out of control. We don't care if it's against law or if they're trying to stop it. We know doctors who are willing to continue and have done so," she said.

NGOs fighting against FGM warn of the "medicalization" of the procedure, in which the barbarism of the practice is whitewashed by the "respectability" that comes from its being performed by trained medical personnel. The London-based NGO Orchid Project, which works to end FGM, has said that one of the most disturbing aspects of the practice in Egypt is the involvement of the medical profession. According to a report by the group:

Although situated in the African continent, Egypt differs from all the other African FGC [female genital cutting] practicing countries. This predominantly refers to the 77% of FGC that is conducted in a medical environment or by a medical professional. The growing rate of FGC medicalisation in Egypt is something that concerns anti-FGC campaigners, particularly when understanding that the rate of medicalisation has risen from 55% to 77% in just over 20 years. This number is a result of the Egyptian government in particular, as they condoned medical FGC and promoted it until 2008. No other FGC practicing country in Africa has experienced the endorsement of their government to practice FGC, and due to the fact Egypt's anti-FGC laws arose as a result of international pressure, it enhances the feelings of tradition and culture in opposition to what is often perceived as neo-colonialism in Egypt regarding anti-FGC campaigns.

Not only does the medicalization of FGM give legitimacy to a harmful practice but it has also added racism to the mix. The Orchid Project quotes a 2011 BBC report from Egypt: "Of medicalisation, community members said how they are advanced and different from 'black Africa' as they aren't practicing FGC in a barbaric or un-hygienic way." Never mind that several of those countries in "black Africa," such as Senegal, had made great progress in radically reducing rates of FGM.

The Orchid Project said that anti-FGM work in Egypt had begun in 1904—that's 110 years of failure. In those 110 years we have "succeeded" in saving just 25 percent of our girls from having their genitals butchered unnecessarily.

I've blamed the Arab world's toxic mix of culture and religion for many of the examples of misogyny I cite in this book. Female genital mutilation is such a difficult practice to eradicate precisely because those two behemoths underpin it. Although both Muslim and Christian girls are subjected to FGM, activists have long complained chiefly of the mosque preachers who instruct their communities that it is their religious duty to cut their daughters.

We Muslims turn ourselves inside out trying to distance ourselves from any Islamic connection to FGM— just as we do with domestic violence—when clearly there are some (too many) who give it a religious justification. Although the Mufti of Egypt joined the Coptic Pope to support the 2008 criminalization and to stress that FGM is required by neither Islam nor Christianity, his words have not sunk in. For some, the Mufti is considered compromised because he's state-appointed, so he is seen as saying whatever the regime wants him to say. For others, his words are one rock thrown against a wall of religious support for FGM.

Muslim scholars have differed on whether any form of genital cutting is required, recommended, or optional based on two controversial sayings by the Prophet. Those sayings are considered weak and of little credibility by some scholars because they seem to be in contradiction to the Qur'an, which itself does not mention any form of genital cutting for women. In fact, passages from the Qur'an and Hadith advocate for women's sexual satisfaction. Both the Qur'an and the Prophet Muhammad discuss foreplay, and describe sex between a husband and a wife as something to be enjoyed by both; the Wasa'il Hadith even states that omitting foreplay is "cruel" (Wasa'il, vol. 14, p. 40). Isn't that Islam, too? Why is it not a religious duty to make sex between a husband and wife enjoyable, and therefore a sin to do anything to prevent such enjoyment, including hacking off the very part of a woman's genitals that would provide her pleasure?

Instead, scholars of the Shafi'i school (one of the four Sunni law schools of Islam) interpret those two dubious Hadiths to allow what is known as the "Sunnah circumcision," in which the prepuce (retractable fold of skin or hood) and/or the tip of the clitoris is removed. That is supposed to be different and distinct from a clitoridectomy and the more severe forms of cutting listed by the

WHO, but as that institution and others stress, any form of the removal of healthy genital tissue is unnecessary and to be considered a mutilation.

When Egypt banned the practice in 2008, some Muslim Brotherhood legislators opposed the law. And some of the movement's officials were on record as doing so until recently. The women's affairs adviser to Mohamed Morsi, Egypt's first president after the overthrow of Mubarak, described FGM as "beautification," and objected to the practice only when it was carried out on girls as young as seven or eight. Parents should wait until their daughters hit puberty, she said. When she made those statements there was, rightly, an outcry. But outcries are hollow and hypocritical unless accompanied by sustained outrage, daily, annually, at the acceptance of FGM in Egypt at large. For some, the outrage was aimed at just the Muslim Brotherhood—attacking only the Muslim Brotherhood's misogyny was a hobby. Many are clearly and willfully blind to the misogyny that flourishes too easily in Egypt no matter who governs. The Muslim Brotherhood never hid its misogyny, but no one should think it holds the copyright on misogyny just because it was so public about it. Egypt's alarmingly high rate of FGM and the medicalization of the practice—with the encouragement of a regime that was not allied with the Muslim Brotherhood—is a reminder that Egyptian approval of FGM extends far beyond foolishly honest statements by the Brotherhood and its members.

Djibouti, Egypt, Mauritania, Somalia, Sudan, and Yemen are the Arab League member countries most associated with FGM, according to a UNICEF study. If we are to stand a chance of further reducing the prevalence of FGM, it is important to take into account the various other countries where the procedure is practiced, how FGM has traveled along with migration to countries outside the areas where it is usually believed to be prevalent (Africa and the Middle East), and what is being done to fight FGM in each region.

In Sudan, where 88 percent of women ages fifteen to forty-nine have suffered FGM (according to UNICEF), there has been no law against the practice since 1983, when the limited ban on the harshest type, implemented under British rule in 1945, was struck down. Sudan is perhaps the nation in the Middle East and North Africa where the practice is most destructive, for there, as in some parts of southern Egypt, infibulation—the most extreme type of FGM, which involves cutting the clitoris and labia minora and sewing together the edges of the labia majora, leaving a hole for menstrual blood and urine—is performed. This type of FGM has the most dire short- and long-term complications, and in many Sudanese communities, this is the only type of FGM that is considered sufficient.

A recent UNICEF campaign against FGM in Sudan

was called Saleema—the Arabic word for "complete," meaning that girls should be left as they were born, with their bodily integrity intact—and employed television and radio spots, billboards, and a pledge to boycott the practice of FGM, which six hundred Sudanese communities have signed since the campaign's launch in 2008. Some activists criticized the campaign's avoidance of the words *cutting* or *FGM*, attributing this to the desire on the part of the organization to appease conservatives who do not want to see the practice eradicated. The campaign's organizers defended their approach, which they say was designed to be inclusive rather than confrontational, and to encourage broad dialogue.

The most persuasive opponents of FGM are the survivors themselves. Nariman, a thirty-five-year-old Egyptian woman who spoke to me for the BBC documentary, said the revolution had changed her mind about FGM. "I'm one of five sisters and we've all had it done to us," she said. "Before the revolution I didn't know it wasn't necessary. It happened to me and I feel like I was done an injustice. I feel it has affected my life and I didn't want this. If I have daughters I will not have this done to them."

Nesma el-Khattab, the young lawyer who works at the Shehab Center, positioned her stance against FGM as part of the revolution as well: "My fight was taken home. My personal revolution began when I was twelve or thirteen. I began to say no to many things in the family. All the women are supposed to wear niqab but I said no to niqab, I fought to go to university, I fought to study law, I fought to work here.

"I fought to work on women's rights—one of my sisters in niqab said, 'As long as you're working in women's rights, it means you've lost faith and gone against God.' If that's the case, so be it because I love my work.

"I fought so I could get all these rights. I fought against cutting, which happened to me when I was nine. I told my family, 'If you do it to my younger sister, I'm going to turn this house upside down.'

"Before, I was saying no. Then the revolution came, and then I began to say, 'I demand!' It's way out there now: head-to-head confrontation. I would go to Tahrir without our family knowing and my mother would say, 'You're not allowed back in the house.' I'm twenty-four. I've been fighting for years but the revolution took it to another level."

That is exactly the connection between the personal and the political, the home and the street, and the street and the state that we must make if we are to save our girls.

The United Nations High Commissioner for Refugees has created a YouTube channel called Too Much Pain, featuring a collection of videos sharing individual stories of FGM. In one video, Djenabou Teliwel Diallo, who was born in Guinea, where the prevalence rate of FGM is 96 percent, tells of her excision, which happened in a large ceremony with a hundred other young girls.

"Everyone was waiting for their turn. I was waiting too and I could hear the screams of the ones who went in before me. Screams. I was just there, frozen. I couldn't run away because it would mean dishonor for my family." Later Djenabou's grandmother attempted a second excision because Djenabou's mother believed the first one had not been done properly. This time, the procedure almost killed Djenabou when her grandmother nicked a vein. Her story is deeply heartbreaking, yet also hopeful: she now lives in Belgium and works as an anti-FGM advocate.

In New York City in 2003, I had the privilege to meet a married couple from Ethiopia and two young sisters from Kenya who had bucked centuries of tradition to say no to FGM. When she got married in 2002 in Kembata, Ethiopia, Genet Girma wore a placard that read "I Am Not Circumcised, Learn from Me." Adisie Abosie, her groom, wore a placard reading "I Am Very Happy to Be Marrying an Uncircumcised Woman." Genet had broken with a rite of passage for girls and young women in that part of Ethiopia in which girls are subjected to what is known as step-two female genital mutilation, or excision: the partial or total removal of the clitoris and the labia minora, with or without excision of the labia majora.

How did Genet and Adisie escape? At their schools, the Kembatta Women's Self-Help Center helped them make the connection between genital mutilation and the difficult childbirths they had seen their mothers suffer.

Genet ran away from home to escape mutilation. Her family, and Adisie's, disowned the couple, but the two persevered and held their wedding in public to spread their message. Some two thousand people attended the ceremony, which was covered extensively by Ethiopia's media. Since their public stand, several other couples have followed suit by publicly rejecting mutilation.

My other two heroes are Edna and Beatrice Kandie, sisters from Kenya. Not only can they happily claim to have saved themselves, four younger sisters, and many other girls from genital mutilation, but they can also boast of changing the law in their country.

After learning from a pastor at their church that the Bible prescribed circumcision for boys only, the sisters told their father they would not undergo the ritual. "Our father was very hostile at first, and we had to run away from home," said Beatrice, fifteen.

After they fled, the sisters contacted the human rights activist and lawyer Ken Wafula, who helped secure a court protection order that forbade their father from forcing them to undergo mutilation. This precedent led to legislation in Kenya that criminalizes female genital mutilation. "Most of our friends and the whole community abandoned us because they didn't like what we were doing," said Beatrice, "but they've accepted us now. Since our case, nobody in our village has been circumcised. I'm happy."

If speaking out against street sexual harassment has long been taboo, then openly discussing FGM has been even further off limits. But it is an especially important, and lifesaving, conversation we must have. Even when FGM is discussed in the Arab world, it is usually under the assumption that it is an "African thing," and its supposed lack of prevalence in the Arabian Peninsula and other parts of Asia, for example, is used to explain its cultural rather than Islamic roots. However, according to the Iraqi German NGO WADI, which has produced a website to document FGM globally called Stop FGM Middle East, genital cutting is not just an "African problem," but has been documented in the Arabian Peninsula and other parts of Asia.

In Saudi Arabia, WADI reports that clinical research about the possible connection between female sexual dysfunction (FSD) and FGM, conducted in 2007–2008, found that of 260 women interviewed at a Jeddah clinic, half of them had been cut. In the Saudi study, the participants are believed to be a mix of Saudi and migrant women, who come from countries more traditionally associated with FGM. Additionally, a study in Kuwait and Saudi Arabia of 4,800 pregnant women found that 38 percent of them had been subjected to FGM. According to an article in the Saudi English-language paper *Arab*

News, "The procedure is rare in regions other than the south of Saudi Arabia but people from that region or from countries that perform it who are living in Saudi Arabia find the people and the place to perform it on their daughters, even though it is not allowed in hospitals and clinics."

Research by students at Dubai Women's College reported that FGM is also practiced in the United Arab Emirates for tribal and Islamic reasons. In their published research, the students said that in a 2002 survey of two hundred students of both sexes, 34 percent of females said they had undergone the procedure. The report included several firsthand accounts of students who recalled when they were cut: some were just babies, and others were seven or eight years old.

The U.S. embassy in the Omani capital, Muscat, held a recent panel discussion on FGM in which it emerged that the practice may be quite widespread in Oman, both in the north and in the southern province of Dhofar. Indonesia, Malaysia, parts of Pakistan and India, and Kurdish areas of northern Iraq also subject girls to FGM. The incident rates of FGM are rarely reported in these countries, most likely because of taboo and silencing. In the absence of official figures, UN bodies such as UNICEF do not include these places among their lists of countries where FGM is practiced.

FGM is also performed in Europe, where the practice continues among some immigrant populations.

FGM may be one of the most prevalent forms of "severe physical child abuse" taking place in Britain, according to the House of Commons Home Affairs Committee. The practice has been outlawed in the United Kingdom since 1985, but the first prosecution for it took place only in 2014. Why have there not been more prosecutions over a practice that threatens an estimated sixty-five thousand girls under the age of thirteen? Members of Parliament accurately ascribe the failure of authorities to deal with FGM to "misplaced concern for cultural sensitivities over the rights of the child." In its report, the committee called this failure to tackle the growing practice of FGM in the United Kingdom a "national scandal" that has resulted in the preventable abuse of thousands of girls.

Again and again, we fail to protect our girls and women. Those who hesitate to criticize genital mutilation out of respect for other cultures should listen to Bogaletch Gebre, director of the Kembatta Women's Self-Help Center, who was cut at the age of six: "When culture affects one's human integrity, when it violates it—be it in terms of gender or in terms of ethnic group—that culture should be condemned, because whenever one of us is hurt or violated, all of us are violated."

It is helpful to remember that clitoridectomy was once practiced in Britain, in the nineteenth century, and in the United States, where articles extolling the virtues of "female circumcision" continued to appear sporadically in medical journals until the 1960s; some of these journals contained "reports of girls or women being sub-jected to various procedures, particularly the shortening of their labia or clitoris when parents or a husband judged them 'too long,' " according to Robert Darby, who has cataloged a history of circumcisions of various kinds.

Darby notes on his website, History of Circumcision, that in Britain the procedure was promoted by Isaac Baker Brown, a mid-Victorian proponent of clitoridec-tomy as a cure for masturbation and nervous complaints. Although his work fell into disgrace, and there were no reliable statistics on clitoridectomy in Britain after the 1860s, the practice seems to have persisted longer in the United States.

A friend told me that after surviving a rape in the early decades of the twentieth century in the United States, her mother was subjected to a clitoridectomy in the hospital, to protect her from "becoming sexually out of control."

I offer those examples not to excuse FGM today—there is no excuse—but to remind readers that various cultures have come up with ways to control women's sexuality and to "beautify" women's genitals, and that just as Western cultures moved beyond the mumbo jumbo that once justified medically altering women's genitals, we in the Middle East and North Africa can (and must) move beyond the cutting of our girls.

Sharing our stories is often the only way we get answers to things we've been too scared to ask. Once, during a conversation about FGM in Egypt that I initiated with a group of women ahead of February 6—the international day of zero tolerance for FGM—a thirty-five-year-old woman asked me a question that was heart-crushing in its simplicity.

"Am I normal? Will I be able to enjoy sex?"

Her cutting was done to her when she was eight at the behest of her grandfather and without the approval or knowledge of her mother, who was not at the house at the time.

I told her that the clitoris was like an iceberg, with the majority of the nerve endings deep in the body and not in the glans. I understood from her question that she was still a virgin and I told her that I hoped when the time came for her to have sex, it would be with a patient man for whom her pleasure was important.

Girls and women are forced to be cultural vectors. Their bodies are the medium upon which culture is engraved, be it through headscarves or cutting. But women are too often barred from authoring the culture that marks them—and only by refusing misogynistic culture can they can become the authors of their own lives. FGM is one of the earliest violations imprinted on the female body, and it is therefore especially harmful.

Reflect on the Dutch Moroccan woman in Amsterdam, the Ethiopian bride and the Kenyan sisters I met in New York City—women's stories make real what is often too easy to dismiss. These brave young women have fought their communities and are reforming their cultures. They have refused to be silenced and have insisted that their own choices, their own narratives, matter.

A male editor I once worked with tried to dissuade me from the personal: "Who cares about what happened to you?" The most subversive thing a woman can do is talk about her life as if it really matters.

It does.

HOME

I called it Home, because I see it as a work that shatters notions of the wholesomeness of the home environment, the household, and the domain where the feminine resides. Having always had an ambiguous relationship with notions of home, family, and the nurturing that is expected out of this situation, I often like to introduce a physical or psychological disturbance to contradict those expectations . . . I see kitchen utensils as exotic objects, and I often don't know what their proper use is. I respond to them as beautiful objects. Being raised in a culture where women have to be taught the art of cooking as part of the process of being primed for marriage, I had an antagonistic attitude to all of that.

—LEBANESE PALESTINIAN MONA HATOUM, INTERVIEWED BY JO GLENCROSS, IN *MONA HATOUM: DOMESTIC DISTURBANCE*, ON HER INSTALLATION "HOME," AT THE TATE MODERN

Lama did not stand a chance. The five-year-old's father, Fayhan al-Ghamdi, was a "cleric," a regular guest on

Muslim television networks despite not being an authorized cleric in Saudi Arabia. He beat Lama with canes, burned her with electrical cables, crushed her skull, and tore off her nails. He also raped her repeatedly, "everywhere," according to a social worker at the hospital where Lama was admitted. It is impossible to imagine what that little girl's last few months alive were like, and it is equally unimaginable that her father inflicted all that torture on her because he apparently suspected the five-year-old was no longer a virgin. She was admitted to the hospital on December 25, 2011, and died a few months later.

A Saudi court sentenced al-Ghamdi to eight years in prison and to eight hundred lashes. Of this term, he served only three months before an Islamic judge overturned the sentence, releasing him. Compare this to the verdict of another Saudi court, which gave four young men sentences of between three and ten years in prison and five hundred to two thousand lashes for dancing naked in public, and gave a verdict of three years in jail to human rights lawyers who were convicted of "disrespecting" the judiciary.

Why this lenient sentence for al-Ghamdi? "Blood money" explains it. Lama's mother accepted a million riyals, roughly $267,000, from her ex-husband as compensation for the next of kin under Islamic law, or Sharia, which is used in lieu of a penal code in Saudi Arabia. By doing so, Lama's mother, a poor single woman with no income, waived her right to demand retribution or justice.

It is worth remembering two things, however: "Blood money" for a female victim, according to Sharia, is half the amount given for a male. And even if Lama's mother had not accepted the money, in Saudi Arabia, where rape and murder are among several crimes punishable by death, a father cannot be executed for murdering his children; nor can husbands be executed for murdering their wives. This is a teaching of Islamic law, the interpretation of which is up to each judge to decide as he passes sentence. Saudi Arabia is the only country in the region that does not have a penal code. Despite the work of activists, including some in the Saudi royal family, justice for Lama's suffering and murder seems unlikely. It is difficult to think of someone more vulnerable than Lama, or someone as powerless to help her as her mother— ex-wife to a "cleric" who just up and decided to take their daughter for a couple of weeks, after which Lama would never return.

Manal Assi also did not stand a chance. Manal was a thirty-three-year-old teacher in Lebanon whose husband bludgeoned her with a pressure cooker after accusing her of adultery. As she lay dying from his blows, Manal's husband, Mohammed Nuheili, called her mother and told her, according to the Associated Press, "Come to your daughter, I am going to kill her."

When Manal's mother arrived at her daughter's home,

she pleaded with Nuheili to let her help her, but he insisted, "I will not let her out. I want her to die in front of you."

Lebanese media reported that neighbors called the police, only to be told they could not interfere in a "family matter." One neighbor told reporters that Nuheili stood at the door to their apartment threatening to shoot anyone who tried to interfere. According to media reports, for two hours Manal's husband would not let paramedics enter their home to tend to her. Manal died soon after she was admitted to the hospital. At the time of this writing, Nuheili has been indicted for premeditated murder and is due to stand trial.

Manal's two daughters say their father beat their mother for years, once to the point of breaking her nose. Like Lama's father, Manal's husband had a second wife, who lived in the same building as Manal, which adds a bitter irony to Nuheili's claim that his wife was seeing another man. Whether you are five or thirty-three, whether it's your father or your husband, men can abuse and kill you and justify it by blaming you for bringing the violence and viciousness upon yourself. As I discussed in a previous chapter, regimes and mobs try hard to push women out of public space and back into the home for their own "safety," knowing full well that, for many women, home can be an even more dangerous place.

Domestic violence is a global scourge and is obviously not a problem exclusively in the Middle East and North

Africa. For too long, women around the world were beaten and killed with little or no protection. But while many nations have made great strides in combating domestic violence, women remain shockingly unprotected throughout the Arab world, due to that same toxic combination of conservative culture, religion, and politics.

Both Lama and Manal were killed before their respective countries had a law criminalizing domestic violence. Yes, both Saudi Arabia and Lebanon, countries that many would place at the opposite ends of the women's rights spectrum, essentially gave men free rein to abuse girls and women and suffer no consequences. For the Arab world, this is not at all unusual.

Only Jordan, Mauritania, and Tunisia have laws that specifically address domestic violence, though these are seldom brought into use. Morocco has an anti-domestic violence law that has waited for years to be passed by parliament. As mentioned earlier, Egypt's penal code allows a man to beat his wife with "good intention." The Iraqi penal code sentences men who kill their wives to serve a maximum of three years in prison rather than life. In Sudan, a strict interpretation of Islam allows domestic abuse, and the law in the United Arab Emirates allows a man to "discipline" his wife and daughters as long as he leaves no marks.

Societal attitudes toward domestic violence are just as forgiving of the violence as regional laws. Many women expect to be beaten, according to the 2008 Egypt

Demographic and Health Survey, which found that 40 percent of women considered beatings justified discipline for a "wrongdoing" such as burning dinner, going out without permission, or withholding sex. Turn on an Arabic-language drama or film, many of which are produced in Egypt, and such views are reflected in the physical abuse against women that is a staple of almost every production.

My father once shared with me a telling anecdote: He and my mother were watching a scholar of Islam whom they respected take viewer questions during a call-in television show. A woman phoned in to tell the scholar that she was still in love with her husband of eleven years and she listed what she said were his virtues. "But he beats me," she said. "What should I do?" The scholar told the woman that if she listed the "pros and cons" of being with her husband, it was clear the good outweighed the bad. The clincher: "What do you do that makes him beat you?"

My father told me that he and my mother were disgusted by the scholar's victim blaming and the fact that he did not say a word chastising the husband for beating his wife. "He never asked the husband, 'Why do you beat her?' and didn't mention at all that the Prophet never beat a woman," my father told me.

In the 2005 Egypt Demographic and Health Survey, 47 percent of women who are or who had ever been married reported being victims of physical violence. In

Tunisia, a 2012 survey showed that 47.2 percent of women had been subjected to physical violence in the home. Over 40 percent of women polled in Lebanon said they had suffered from physical abuse, a third reported sexual abuse, nearly two-thirds were victims of verbal abuse, and 19 percent said they had experienced emotional abuse. The researchers behind the Lebanese survey, conducted at American University of Beirut Medical Center, spoke about their respondents' attitude toward abuse: "Many abused women are totally resigned to their situation and decide to stay in an abusive relationship because of the fear of losing their children, the need to conform to social expectations, the lack of financial independence, the lack of family support, and the duty to obey their spouses."

Alongside those reasons, many women stay in abusive situations simply because they have nowhere else to go. The majority of countries in the region do not have shelters for girls and women who want to escape violent homes. Even if they wanted to flee, for girls and women especially, it is a huge taboo to leave home under any circumstances. The majority of young men and women in the region live with their parents until they marry.

Recent attempts to criminalize and discourage domestic violence in Saudi Arabia and Lebanon highlight the disparity between the two countries, and the fact that laws alone cannot change a societal problem. In August 2013 the Saudi Arabian cabinet passed a draft law criminalizing domestic abuse. The unprecedented "Protection from Abuse" law sets down a prison sentence of up to one year and up to 50,000 riyals ($13,300) in fines for those found guilty of committing psychological or physical abuse.

The law was passed four months after a local charity, the King Khalid Foundation, launched a first-of-its-kind campaign to raise awareness about violence against women. The campaign's poster, which was widely circulated on social media, featured a woman in a face veil, with just her eyes showing, one of which was blackened. The caption under the image read "Some Things Can't Be Covered—Fighting Women's Abuse Together."

Some local activists praised the passing of the law as a sign that the kingdom was finally taking violence against women seriously—and violence against not just female family members but also domestic workers, who are sometimes brutalized by their employers. As the Reuters news agency pointed out, before the law, "domestic violence against women, children or domestic workers was treated under a general penal code based on Islamic sharia law. Judges were left to decide according to their understanding of sharia codes, which were seen as permitting mild application of violence against 'disobedient' wives and generally treated domestic violence as a private matter."

Yet Human Rights Watch criticized the law for not detailing "specific enforcement mechanisms to ensure prompt investigations of abuse allegations or prosecution of those who commit abuses."

"Saudi Arabia has finally banned domestic abuse, but has yet to say which agencies will police the new law. Without effective mechanisms to punish domestic abuse, this law is merely ink on paper," said Joe Stork, HRW's deputy director for the Middle East and North Africa.

The Saudi enshrinement of male privilege further mitigates any good the law can provide for women. According to HRW:

> The law defines abuse as bodily, psychological, or sexual, but does not make explicit that marital rape is a crime, leaving open the possibility of differing interpretations of criminality. The law also does not address institutional systems that grant male family members and employers inordinate power over their female relatives or domestic workers, such as Saudi Arabia's male guardianship system and unfair worker sponsorship regulations. In many cases, dependents would require logistical support or transportation from male relatives or employers, who themselves often are the abusers, in order to report abuses or escape abusive situations.

Just as Egyptians must turn to a predatory police force to file complaints of abuse, women in Saudi Arabia are dependent on the very same family members who might be their abusers to help them report abuse. It is imperative to continue to condemn Saudi Arabia for refusing to confront this institutionalized misogyny. All this new law does is allow Saudi Arabia to boast that it has anti–domestic abuse legislation on the books—a hollow "accomplishment."

Human Rights Watch: "Saudi women and migrant domestic workers who report violations such as rape sometimes face counteraccusations of fornication, leaving them open to criminal prosecution. Parents can pursue criminal prosecutions against their dependents on the charge of 'uquq, or 'parental disobedience.' Saudi Arabia needs to abolish such practices if the new law is to be effective."

Furthermore, as Khaled al-Fakher, secretary general of the government-licensed National Society for Human Rights, told Reuters, one reason domestic violence was rampant in Saudi Arabia was because tribal traditions prevented women from reporting abuse for fear of social stigma. "Women think what the community would say about her if she filed a complaint," he said.

The same victim shaming also silenced women in Lebanon from speaking out against domestic violence for years. It took seven years of lobbying by the local

NGO KAFA (which means "Enough") and media coverage of several horrific incidents of domestic violence before the Lebanese parliament finally passed the landmark Protection of Women and Family Members from Domestic Violence draft bill in April 2014—almost a year after Saudi Arabia passed its law.

One difference in the circumstances of each country's domestic violence bill is quite telling. In Lebanon, to put pressure on lawmakers to finally pass the draft bill, KAFA organized a protest in the capital, Beirut, on International Women's Day (March 8, 2014) to demand a law to protect women from domestic abuse. The NGO's call for the march included a moving video plea on YouTube by mothers of several women who had been killed by their abusive husbands. Some of those mothers marched hand in hand at the head of a group of around five thousand, carrying photographs of their daughters. It was one of the largest demonstrations for a social issue in Lebanon. Many of the protesters carried banners accusing judges and forensic experts of falsifying reports on domestic violence deaths. I have not heard of any other such marches against domestic violence in the Arab world.

It is this readiness to speak out—mothers talking openly about what happened to their daughters—that makes women killed as a result of domestic abuse more than just initials in media reports. A reminder of Audre Lorde's insistence on speaking: "Your silence will not save you."

Unlike Saudi Arabia, Lebanon has some shelters for women who choose to leave abusive homes. In 2013, KAFA and the Internal Security Forces launched a nationwide billboard campaign encouraging women to report domestic abuse, according to Al Jazeera English. That same year, women's rights group Resource Center for Gender Equality (ABAAD) opened the first of three halfway houses for women in Lebanon, and in November 2013, KAFA launched a scheme to educate police on how to protect women from domestic violence. According to *The Guardian*, KAFA says it receives more than twenty-six hundred calls to its domestic abuse help line each year. We need exactly such initiatives if our laws are to move beyond "ink on paper."

Human Rights Watch called Lebanon's draft law good but incomplete. Among its positive aspects is that it allows women to seek restraining orders against their abusers. But how seriously police will take such an order remains to be seen, considering general police reluctance to interfere in what they consider "family business."

The most disturbing aspect of Lebanon's draft anti–domestic violence law is that not only did legislators remove the criminalization of marital rape that KAFA fought so hard to keep in the bill, but worse, the bill introduces the notion of a "marital right to intercourse."

"This is a very big setback," KAFA cofounder Ghada Jabbour told *The Guardian*. "They [the politicians considering the bill] felt pressure to re-put in a provision about marital rape, but what they put in criminalizes the use of threats or force in order to get what they call 'the marital right.' The use of force is criminalized anyway by the penal code in Lebanon. This is just playing with words . . . the use of the 'marital right' is a very new and religious concept within our civil law."

Criminalizing marital rape "could lead to the imprisonment of the man," Sheikh Ahmad al-Kurdi, a judge in the Sunni religious court, told CNN, "where in reality he is exercising the least of his marital rights."

In Lebanon, domestic violence cases are typically heard in the religious courts, the judicial authorities that preside over each of the country's eighteen sects and faith communities under a set of laws known as "personal status laws," which govern divorce, child custody, and other domestic issues. The priority of those courts is the preservation of the family, not the protection of girls and women from violence.

Dar al-Fatwa, Lebanon's top Sunni authority, and the Higher Shi'a Islamic Council both said they opposed the draft anti–domestic abuse bill on the basis that they believed Islamic law sufficiently protected the status of women and so should remain the basis for governing legal issues related to Muslim families. According to Al Jazeera English, Dar al-Fatwa condemned the draft law in a 2011 statement for "disintegrating Muslim families in Lebanon and preventing children from being raised according to Islam, in addition to causing a conflict of competences between the concerned civil and Islamic courts."

Clearly, in Lebanon, a country of Muslims and Christians, conservative lawmakers agreed to the notion that religious authority must have the last word on the domestic sphere. The veneer of liberal social attitudes in Lebanon is deceptive. All eighteen of Lebanon's personal status laws discriminate against women, in effect trapping them in violent marriages, according to Rothna Begum, women's rights researcher for the Middle East and North Africa region at Human Rights Watch.

In the first conviction since Lebanon's parliament passed the draft law, a man was jailed for nine months and fined 20 million Lebanese pounds ($13,258) for a brutal assault on his wife. Nonetheless, the wife, who said her husband beat her every week during their marriage of eighteen months, had to seek a divorce through religious courts, a challenge that a women's rights activist called a "long battle."

Why should a woman who has been beaten weekly and whose husband is finally held accountable still struggle to free herself? Let's take a closer look at the patriarch's laws, or what are known as personal status laws, the minefield of misogyny and injustice that governs marriage, divorce, child custody, and inheritance in the Muslim world. The laws that govern family life are decided by the interpretation of your religion, but you can be sure of one thing: they guarantee that men and their interests are always paramount.

The legal codes of most countries in the region have been "modernized" in the last century, either through laws imposed by colonial rule or through a move away from religiously based legislation and toward secular laws. For example, even when a country's constitution states— as many in the region do—that Sharia is one of the sources from which law is drawn, none of them, with the exception of Saudi Arabia's, allow for the amputation of hands as a punishment for theft, although Sharia stipulates such a punishment.

Why is it acceptable to move beyond Sharia when it comes to theft but impossible to do so when it comes to women's rights in the family? The simple answer: personal status laws are the area where religious and conservative men shore up their control of women's lives.

Such tenacious insistence on keeping women bound by ancient codes is not specific to Islam. In predominantly Muslim countries, where several religions are practiced, everyone is subject to the same laws except in the case of family laws, which are dictated by one's religion or sect. In Egypt, for example, Christians are subject to canonical law when it comes to marriage and divorce, child custody, and so on, while Muslims must follow Egypt's interpretation of Islam. In the absence of a civil law governing such family issues, what ends up happening is that women and children are subject to ideas that were first formulated centuries ago. A woman's religion or sect might be different, but her subjugation to laws that favor men is the same.

Take the example of the United Arab Emirates, as described by the International Federation for Human Rights (FIDH):

> Prior to the adoption of the Personal Status Code in 2005, the areas of personal status and family were regulated by Sharia law. The new Personal Status Code contains numerous discriminatory provisions. For example, under Article 39 of the Personal Status Code, a woman's male guardian and her prospective husband are the parties to the marital contract (the validity of the contract is contingent upon the woman's approval and signature). Under Article 56, wives are required to obey their husbands, take care of the house, and raise the children.
>
> Concerning divorce, women can only request a divorce from the courts under the Khul procedure, under Article 110 of the Personal Status Code. Under this procedure, she must renounce all her financial rights under the marriage contract, most notably, her dowry, or *mahr*.
>
> Concerning custody of children, women are only considered to be the physical guardians. They have the right to custody up to the age of thirteen for girls and

age ten for boys, after which custody can be reassessed
by the family courts. If a woman chooses to remarry,
she automatically forfeits her rights to custody of her
children from her previous marriage. Polygamy is authorized [for men].

The Personal Status Code also ensures that women
inherit half the amount that men inherit, and makes it
much easier for a man to obtain a divorce—according
to the FIDH report, women who leave their husbands
can be required by law to return. This, combined with
age-related child custody, creates an emotional terrorism
that keeps wives in abusive marriages.

Depending on which Islamic school of thought a
country follows, personal status laws stipulate that a
woman needs the permission of a male guardian to
marry, even if she is a widow or divorcée. (The Maliki
school of Islamic jurisprudence, followed by the UAE,
makes such a stipulation.) Two recent cases documented
by the UAE-based newspaper *The National* highlight the
infantilization of women that this law engenders.

A fifty-one-year-old Emirati divorcée told *The National* that she was considering traveling to another
country rather than taking her twenty-six-year-old son
to court to obtain his approval of her remarriage. The
second case was even more surreal—that of a forty-year-
old whose eleven-year-old son would become the arbiter

of her remarriage once he reached the age of puberty. "This law is a disgrace. I'm a grown woman and should be allowed to make my own decisions," she said.

Nonetheless, two male lawyers that the newspaper interviewed insisted that the guardianship system was in the best interest of the women. One, Dr. Shakir Al Marzouqi, a legal consultant in the UAE, actually went so far as to say "men know better": "In the bigger picture it is the men who know more and a woman's father, brother, or son cares for her interest more than her own self."

Fortunately, a female lawyer made clear to *The National* just how open to abuse the guardianship system is. Aisha al-Tenajii, a legal consultant, told *The National* that the legal office where she worked had been involved in numerous cases of legal guardians preventing a woman from getting married for questionable reasons, including because the prospective bridegroom was from a "family considered unequal in social status" or was not a UAE national.

But even with this knowledge, al-Tenajii would not say that the guardianship system should be scrapped altogether as unfair and infantilizing to women. Rather, she suggested that after a certain age, a woman should be allowed to marry without the approval of a guardian: "We are not asking for it to be removed. After all, there should be some regulation, but not like in the case of the

51-year-old woman. After the age of 25, for example, a woman who was previously married should not require a guardian to remarry."

We are so socialized in our oppression that even in the face of injustice, we know to stay within the lines. Instead of a bold demand for the removal of a system that keeps women forever at the whim of male guardians, even their adolescent sons, women meekly suggest reform.

One law in the UAE takes this absurdity further, by making women the property not only of their sons, but of their babies! According to a law passed in 2014, a mother's breasts are her child's property. A clause that is part of the child's rights laws makes it mandatory for a mother to breastfeed her child for two years, opening the way for husbands to sue their wives if they don't breastfeed for the stipulated time. This in a country that gives mothers just one month of maternity leave and where existing regulations ordering offices to provide nurseries so that working mothers can breastfeed have never been enforced.

A member—male, of course—of the UAE's Federal National Council, which passed the law, said that it aimed to make breastfeeding "a duty and not an option" for able mothers. The council suggested that wet-nurses be provided for children whose mothers had died or could not feed them, but it did not say who should pay for these wet-nurses.

With a few exceptions, these provisions are very similar to their counterparts in other countries in the region. Put crudely, marriage ensures that a woman, after a childhood and youth of obedience to her father, shifts that obedience to her husband, for whom she becomes a baby maker and wet-nurse to his children (for the children essentially belong to the father).

Women's rights groups in several countries have fought for years to mitigate the discrimination of personal status laws. After a decades-long battle by feminists in Egypt, parliament in 2000 ratified the "Khul procedure," in which a woman who wants a divorce must renounce her financial rights under the marriage contract. But in Egypt today it is apparent that only affluent women can afford to renounce such rights to obtain a divorce. Poor women have little recourse to leave abusive marriages, and yet the personal status laws that allow such injustices to continue are treated as if they were a religious revelation in and of themselves, untouchable and unrelated to the lives of the women they harm.

When the role and the use of religion in the continued oppression and abuse of girls and women is starkly presented, I often hear from my fellow Muslims: "But this isn't the fault of Islam. It is the fault of Muslims who abuse religion." Then they usually launch into how perfect everything would be if we practiced "the proper Islam." Never mind that the clerics in Lebanon who opposed the anti–domestic violence bill fully believed they were advocating for a "proper Islam," and had the weight of the establishment on their side. We are in denial if we do not honestly reckon with the role of religion in maintaining the patriarch's rule at home, including how the men of religion help him to uphold his rule. The "proper Islam" defense serves only the rule of the patriarch. Our best chance for pushing back against such idealized notions is to offer examples from the lived realities of girls and women. Those who insist on holding on to the ideal will remind us over and over again that the Prophet's last sermon emphasized love and respect for women. But has that teaching made its way into personal status laws?

I learned the importance of the term *lived realities* in Kuala Lumpur, Malaysia, at the launch of Musawah (the Arabic word for "equality"), a global movement for equality and justice in the Muslim family. Bringing together activists and scholars of Islam who promote a progressive interpretation of the religion, Musawah focuses much of its work on personal status laws. The scholars who belong to Musawah (women and men) have long advocated a progressive reinterpretation of Islam to mitigate the injustices I list in this chapter.

I am most interested in the female scholars, inside and outside Musawah, who have struggled for years to wrest the power of interpretation from men. For example, I learned of a South African scholar—who does not work with Musawah but whose religious circle focuses on challenging religiously fueled misogyny—whose students have crossed out from their copies of the Qur'an a verse that has been interpreted to allow men to beat "disobedient" wives. For many, this alteration of a sacred text is tantamount to blasphemy. In another case, an Iranian American woman has issued the first English translation of the Qur'an by a woman and has handled that verse by providing what she believes are alternative meanings to the word that is taken to mean "to beat." Others say that regardless of the original meaning of the verse, the fact that Muhammad never beat a woman should be taken as an example, and the concepts of justice and mercy articulated in the Qur'an should take precedence over one verse allowing corporal punishment for "disobedient" wives.

Amina Wadud, a mentor and personal hero of mine, puts it simply when she asks, "God is just—do these interpretations uphold that spirit of justice?"

I am tempted at times to say that any woman who chooses to get married in our part of the world, knowing the personal status laws that work against her well-being and that of her future daughters, must be insane or a masochist. Yet that would be to forget that, for economic and social reasons, the choice to reject marriage is not available to most women. Whether it is for the economic support a husband provides or the ability to have socially sanctioned sex without risking the wrath of the god of virginity, marriage is not going anywhere. News articles have occasionally trumpeted an emerging class of young, hypereducated women who make more money than their male counterparts and who don't "need" a husband for the reasons their mothers or grandmothers did, but they remain a minority, cushioned by privilege that is unavailable to most women in the region. It is a form of denial to act shocked that "even educated" women cave in to and perpetuate patriarchal values. Even worse, it negates the right of women who have not been fortunate enough to receive an education to demand a life that is free of the injustice of misogyny. Every woman in our region deserves equality and respect.

To choose to rebel, to disobey, comes at a great cost (not least social) that not everybody is able to pay. To be ostracized by one's family in a society that places so much emphasis on social ties is a terrible and dangerous thing. In our culture, marriage and motherhood are deified, raised up as the ultimate female experience. But for what? When a mother's breasts are being regulated for the sake of the child, and yet the mother herself hardly has any safeguards to protect her, what is she but an incubator for offspring and breasts for their sustenance?

She is also vagina on demand. Tunisia and Mauritania are the only countries in the region that have a law against marital rape, though these are rarely enforced due to loopholes that allow charges to be dropped if the victim withdraws her case.

Attitudes toward rape across the Arab world are abysmal. The stigma (and often the law) is much harsher on the woman than on the rapist. Women often keep quiet rather than risk arousing blame or humiliation, or being raped again at a police station. In some cases, they risk being killed by a relative to rid the family of shame. Precise statistics are unavailable—in part because rape victims can themselves be prosecuted under *zina*, the area of Islamic law governing unlawful sexual inter-course. Victim services in most countries are provided by NGOs rather than the state, according to a 2010 re-port by the UN Committee on the Elimination of Dis-crimination against Women.

In Libya, under the forty-two years of the Qaddafi regime, women accused of violating "moral codes" were locked up in "social rehabilitation" centers. The only way for women and girls to leave those centers was if a male relative took them into custody or if the women married. Human Rights Watch said most of those women went to the centers against their will, and those who went of their own volition did so because Libya had no shelters for survivors of violence.

Other countries turn rape into wedlock by allowing rapists to escape conviction by marrying their victims. Some of the countries in the region had such legislation introduced during colonial times by their occupiers. An article in the Moroccan penal code was based on a simi-lar measure in France, which was repealed in 1994.

Morocco was a protectorate of France until 1956. Amina Filali and Amina Tamiri were two Moroccan teenagers (both sixteen, although some reports put Tamiri at twelve) forced to marry the men who'd raped them. Filali committed suicide in 2012; Tamiri, in 2013. In January 2014, after intensive lobbying by rights activists, Morocco amended the article in its penal code (Article 475) that allowed rapists of underage girls to avoid prosecution by marrying their victims.

Rights groups welcomed the amendment but said that a complete overhaul of Morocco's penal code was needed to ensure the protection of girls and women in the country, where (as in many countries across the region) rape is such a taboo that families hush it up or force survivors to marry, and where child marriage persists.

I despise the word *victim*. I've never called myself a victim of sexual assault. I'm a survivor, and so is every girl and woman who survives the crime of sexual violation. But there is no word other than *victim* to describe Amina Filali and Amina Tamiri. How do you survive a marriage to your rapist? Trapped in a state of perpetual victimhood as the wife of your rapist, where is the chance to heal, to mourn, to grieve over what happened to you, to overcome and overpower the trauma, when your rapist is there with you every day? It does not bear thinking about. There is no survival. The two girls' suicides underline that.

Listen to Dalal, who was just sixteen when she was

forced to marry her rapist. Dalal is from Jordan, where Article 308 of the penal code allows rapists to escape punishment if they marry their victims. She spoke to us in March 2014 for the BBC World Service radio documentary *Women of the Arab Spring*. In 2012 her assailant kidnapped and raped her and then held her against her will for five days. She escaped. A judge sentenced her rapist to twenty-three years for rape and armed kidnapping, and for drugging Dalal, but he told Dalal's assailant that if he persuaded her to marry him, he could get out of the sentence. Dalal initially refused to marry him, but then gave in under pressure from her rapist's parents and her own.

"When I married him it was like he was raping me again because I didn't want him. I didn't want to get married, and he raped me and hit me and burnt me with cigarettes and his parents would encourage him to do these things," she said.

When Dalal spoke to us for the documentary, she had returned to her parents' home pregnant and intending to get a divorce.

"Girls like me, their position in society is different from their parents and other people. I'm against the idea that someone who is raped then gets married to her rapist. But the girl doesn't have any other option because she'll forever be ostracized by all society," Dalal said.

For *Women of the Arab Spring*, I went with producer Gemma Newby to Jordan to see what effect, if any, the

mass uprisings had had on the kingdom, which remained under the rule of King Abdullah. Jordan might
not have had its own revolution, but it had felt the ripples
of those nearby. There were protests over the economy,
and women's groups had come out on the streets to protest child marriage laws, so-called honor killings, and
domestic violence. Subsequent political reform brought
in a 12 percent quota for women in parliament, and
there are now eighteen female parliamentarians. One
of those women lawmakers, Wafa Ben Mostafa, heads a
campaign to abolish Article 308. I asked her if Jordanian
women could successfully push for its repeal in the way
their Moroccan counterparts had fought Article 475.

"It will not be surprising when I say to you that every
woman member of parliament attended the session for
signing the petition and none of them opposed, and this
indicates that more women in parliament will naturally
lead to there being better laws for women. Twenty-two
members have signed the petition to cancel this law,
but it is difficult to do so because there are various legislators and jurists and men in parliament who think this
article preserves the structure of Jordanian society and
protects the social fabric," Ben Mostafa told me.

Yet as Dalal's case painfully makes clear, Article 308
doesn't protect girls and women from the men who rape
them; in many cases, it does the very opposite.

Eva Abu Halaweh, a lawyer and executive director of
Mizan, a center that, among other things, advocates for

the rights of girls and women who suffer the consequences of Article 308, told me there was no mechanism for the attorney general in Jordan to follow up on cases such as that of Dalal, whom Mizan repesents.

According to an article in *Al Arabiya News*, weddings arranged under Article 308 must last for five years for the rapist to be guaranteed immunity against future prosecution. Abu Halaweh said it was hard to know how many cases there were of girls or women marrying their rapists, because Article 308 is not referred to in marriage contracts. But a September 2014 article in *The Jordan Times* estimated that as many as 95 percent of rape cases in Jordan are resolved with the survivors marrying their rapists.

Such marriages, Abu Halaweh said, aren't "real marriage in practice because a woman's will wasn't taken into consideration; it's usually pressure from family, and sometimes they receive money, a high dowry. Some people think it's for the benefit of women, but usually she doesn't benefit."

Abu Halaweh said that Article 308 pushed women between "two false choices": "to save your life from honor crime you marry your rapist. If you don't, you face a life-threatening crime from your own family." She told me of women placed in protective custody and girls placed in juvenile centers in order to protect them from relatives who intended to kill them to rid the family of the "shame" of their rape.

To further complicate the ramifications of Article 308, and to illustrate how the ban on extramarital sex forces women into ridiculous options, Abu Halaweh said that sometimes Article 308 was invoked by girls under the age of eighteen who wanted to marry their boyfriends but could not obtain their families' approval, and that couples caught having sex are pressured into Article 308 marriages by their families.

Why does Jordan still have Article 308? I asked Abdel Moneim Odat, the head of the legal committee in the Jordanian parliament.

"The reason we don't punish the crime is in order to protect the family, the girl in general, her parents, and her reputation, because when a girl gets married the social impact of the crime disappears," he said. "We would have to look at studies and statistics—legislation is a social need which expresses the wishes of a particular society—it springs from traditions, customs, and beliefs. The law cannot be separated from this."

Article 308 makes it clear that Jordan desperately needs to have a conversation on sexual freedom, shame, and honor. Legislation should set, and not follow, the example. Dalal's mother now realizes that Jordan continues to reward rapists while punishing their victims: "I regret the day I helped him get off the twenty-three-year sentence," she said, "because he and boys like him think, 'She'll marry me and I'll get off the punishment.' He robbed her of her treasure, she'll never get it back, it won't be like it was for her before this happened. This raping and marrying the victim is wrong."

Nothing more horrifically epitomizes marital rape than child marriage, which a 2010 UNICEF report defines as a marriage in which one of the participants is under eighteen years of age. This sorry practice is permitted and prevalent not just in poor countries such as Sudan, Yemen, and my own, Egypt, but also in much wealthier Saudi Arabia.

In Sudan, girls can legally marry as soon as they reach puberty. In Yemen and Saudi Arabia there is no minimum age for marriage. According to Human Rights Watch and Yemeni government data from 2006, 52 percent of girls are married before they turn eighteen (often to much older men) and 14 percent before age fifteen. Witness the case of Rawan, an eight-year-old Yemeni girl who was killed by her "husband." She died of internal bleeding after a man five times her age fucked her to death on their "wedding night."

When an eight-year-old is effectively sold off by impoverished parents to a forty-year-old man, the use of terms such as *marriage* and *husband* is an abomination. While a Dubai-based news organization claims that the story is a hoax and has circulated a video of a little girl who is allegedly Rawan, alive and well, the Yemeni journalist who originally reported the story stands by it, accusing local officials of a cover-up. There's no denying that global outrage over the story has brought scrutiny to the prevalence of child brides in Yemen and throughout the region, opening an important dialogue. Hooria Mashhour, Yemen's human rights minister, made a statement acknowledging this to CNN: "This isn't the first time a child marriage has happened in Yemen, so we should not focus only on this case. Many child marriages take place every year in Yemen. It's time to end this practice."

Human Rights Watch identified the political and constitutional transition taking place in Yemen as an important opportunity to secure protection for women's and girls' rights, recommending that the minimum age of marriage be set at eighteen. SEYAJ, a Yemeni children's rights group, issued a similar request. It remains to be seen at the time of this writing whether such a recommendation will make it into Yemen's yet-to-be written constitution; how, further down the line, it will be enforced; and if religious and tribal leaders will accept it.

Some Yemeni girls are sold into marriage by families who cannot afford to take care of them. But poverty is not the only motivator behind child marriage and its supporters. UNICEF identifies the gender discrimination inherent in social attitudes as a contributing factor. Such discrimination makes sure boys get preferential access to education while girls begin their primary task of procreation. Some ultraconservative Salafists in Egypt were keen on getting rid of a minimum age of marriage. My book focuses on Arabic-speaking countries of the

Middle East and North Africa, but it is worth remembering that one of the first things Ayatollah Khomeini did after the 1979 Iranian Revolution was to remove the minimum age of marriage as part of his push to revise all law in accordance with Sharia.

When Yemeni activists tried to ban child marriage in 2010, some of the country's most influential Islamic leaders declared that those who opposed child marriage were "apostates." They understood that such a decree would make it difficult if not impossible for parliament to approve legislation setting a minimum age of seventeen for marriage. Even more disturbing was the number of Yemeni women who followed the teachings of those religious leaders and who showed up in the capital to protest the child marriage ban, carrying signs that read, "Yes to the Islamic Rights of Women."

Whose Islam deems the "marriage"—or, rather, the de facto rape of girls as young as eight—a "right"? Certainly not mine, nor that of many other Muslims. Yet these influential religious leaders, these ultraconservatives and proponents of child marriage, use what they say is the example of the Prophet's marriage to one of his wives, Aisha, to justify child marriage. They cite that example knowing that many people will be afraid to appear critical of anything the Prophet is believed to have done—hence the labeling of those who oppose child marriage as "apostates."

If they are so eager to follow what they believe was

Muhammad's marriage to a child—Aisha's age has been disputed, with varying accounts putting it at nine and others at nineteen—why are they not as eager to follow the example of his first marriage? Khadijah, a rich divorcée and Muhammad's senior by fifteen years, employed Muhammad and proposed to him. While Khadijah was alive, Muhammad was not married to any other woman. Muslims are taught she was the first person to believe in Muhammad when he told her he had received a revelation. So are our esteemed clerics ready to follow that example and advocate marrying older women? Look around and try to find a modern-day Khadijah. Why has the notion of the child bride persisted, but not the older spouse modeled by Khadijah? Most of Muhammad's wives were older than him. Why are our clerics not advocating marrying older women as sunnah, the example of Muhammad that Muslims are encouraged to emulate.

The simple answer is because Khadijah represents the power and autonomy that some clerics despise in women. The child bride is helpless, malleable, without experience of any kind, and lacking any ability to challenge a man's authority. So those clerics who insist on the "Islamic right" to marry little girls should just be honest about it: they want malleable and powerless girls who will never challenge them. We must say no once and for all by outlawing such marriages and seeing them for what they are: pedophilia. The protection of our girls must take priority over the fragile egos of clerics and of those men whom clerics give the green light to sexually abuse girls. Regardless of how old Aisha was when Muhammad married her, we must have the guts to say that marriages in the seventh century were one thing and marriages in 2014 are another, and that today it is a crime to marry little girls. We must be unequivocal in this.

Rawan reportedly died after she was *raped*, just as Lama died after she was *raped*. Until child marriage is put in those terms, until we stop using euphemisms to water down what we do to our girls, more prepubescent girls will die from internal bleeding from the trauma of sex on their little bodies. More girls will die like Fawziya Ammodi, twelve, another Yemeni, who died in 2009 from severe bleeding after struggling for three days in labor. Her baby also died.

Slavish obedience to the clerics, who know how to squeeze every last drop of advantage out of religion, is killing our girls. We must speak—blaspheme, if necessary; be accused of being apostates, if that is what is required. Muslims are taught that Islam put an end to the Arabian practice of burying alive newborn baby girls because they were considered worthless and a burden, but as long as we stay quiet in the face of the abomination of child marriage, we are effectively burying our girls alive today.

There was a moment in Egypt in 2014, as a three-month-long curfew in provinces across the country kept people at home for most of the evening and all of the night, when the patriarch at home and the patriarch in the presidential palace were mirror images. As more and more people began to chafe at an effective house arrest, it could have been an opportunity for the boys and men of the country to reflect on the fact that house arrest is the reality in the lives of the women they know. Most Egyptian families impose a curfew of some sort on their female members, especially the unmarried ones.

Some men to whom I suggested the connection scoffed. I asked them to consider how frustrated their sisters or female friends were by a curfew that would not be soon lifted. I reminded them that while the "father of the nation" was about to lift the curfew he had imposed on the country, the father at home would be keeping his curfew in place.

I lost count of the number of "yes, but" replies I received. Some men explained why the curfew imposed on girls and women at home was correct and should continue while the curfew imposed on the country had gone on too long and should be lifted. A range of excuses—from "What will people say if a girl comes home in the middle of the night?" to "It's not safe out there for girls"—was offered as justification. Perhaps the saddest response came from a young Egyptian woman, currently studying in the United Kingdom and present in the audience at the taping of the Al Jazeera English television program I took part in called *Head to Head*. She insisted that her father didn't hate her and that the reason he imposed a curfew on her was out of concern and to protect her.

"Protect you from what?" I asked her.

She answered, of course, that her father was protecting her from the men on the streets. This begs the question: Why don't we ever consider imposing a curfew on boys and men as a way of protecting girls and women from the harm men do them in public? The very idea is, to many, laughable. But it is time to present the issue in such stark terms, and it is time either to oppose both curfews—from the patriarch outside, on the whole country, and the patriarch inside, on only girls and women— or else be called hypocrites.

Several times, when discussing misogyny in the region, I have heard: "But the women [Egyptian, Saudi, Moroccan, etc.] are so strong. They're the real powers at home."

Who are these strong women who run their homes? Lama's mother certainly wasn't one of them. Manal Assi in Beirut wasn't, either. The notion of the strong woman at home is a myth we are encouraged to believe in order to keep in place an oppressive system, in order to deflect the question of injustice and inequality. The "strong woman" at home cannot advance herself if she has internalized patriarchy and its ills.

That myth reminds me of bell hooks's description in her 1981 book *Ain't I a Woman? Black Women and Feminism* of the romanticization of the Black female experience:

> When feminists acknowledge in one breath that black women are victimized and in the same breath emphasize their strength, they imply that though black women are oppressed they manage to circumvent the damaging impact of oppression by being strong—and that is simply not the case. Usually, when people talk about the 'strength' of black women they are referring to the way in which they perceive black women coping with oppression. They ignore the reality that to be strong in the face of oppression is not the same as overcoming oppression, that endurance is not to be confused with transformation.

Repeating, meaninglessly, that women "run their homes" is a cop-out, an abdication of the responsibility to speak out and to condemn the institutionalized misogyny of personal status laws that permeates every aspect of the female experience in the region.

Gloria Anzaldúa, bell hooks, and other women who've critiqued their cultures and communities were attacked for doing so, but their insistence on those critiques inspires me, and their courage in the face of such attacks—

many from men who didn't want outsiders to see "dirty linen"—reminds me that it's only through such critiques that we stand a chance of overthrowing the patriarchs in our homes and in our minds.

It is often the power and rage of personal storytelling that can begin those necessary revolutions. The power of women's stories lies in their ability to tear down the soundproof walls of home. Sometimes those stories just need an open mic to finally be heard. In the summer of 2012, on a stage set up in the garden of an arts gallery in the middle of an old working-class Cairo neighborhood, a young woman took the mic.

"I can't tell you this while facing you so I'm going to turn around and then share my story," she said and proceeded to tell us, as her back was turned to us, that when she was eleven years old, a cleric her parents had hired to teach her Qur'anic recitation sexually abused her.

Courage, vulnerability, grace.

Her revelation followed a performance by a theater group that collects oral narratives from women to stage. That night's performance by Bussy—the Arabic word for "look"—was on the theme of the street sexual harassment that women are subjected to in Egypt. After Bussy's show, the open mic initiative Project Mareekh (meaning "Mars") set up. The premise of their piece was simple: Sign up and take your turn to say whatever you want. No one is allowed to interrupt you. The initiative has taken its open mic to various places and settings as a way of encouraging freedom of expression, to inspire Egyptians to find their voice and speak.

I have never before (or since) heard an Egyptian woman speak about being subjected to childhood sex abuse. Those of us in the audience were stunned. Several people hugged her after she got off the stage. After a few other speakers took the open mic, another young woman, this one facing us, told us how when she was fourteen a friend of her father's sexually abused her and she went on to connect her suicide attempts and psychological problems to that abuse.

This courage is the same as that which fuels women to speak out against the sexual violence they've experienced on the street. As risky as it is to speak publicly about street sexual harassment and assault, though, speaking out against sex abuse, speaking out against the crimes that go on in the home, is riskier. Home is where the hurt is, and home is where we must start to heal.

ROADS THROUGH THE DESERT

"But I will not glorify those aspects of my culture which
injured me and which have injured me in the name of protecting me."

—GLORIA ANZALDÚA, *BORDERLANDS/LA FRONTERA:*

THE NEW MESTIZA

In 1990, forty-seven Saudi women famously violated the
kingdom's ban on female drivers by taking to the wheel
in a convoy through Riyadh, the capital city. They were
denounced as whores in mosques, banned from working for two years, and had their passports temporarily
confiscated.

Saudi Arabia, which fuels so many of the world's cars
with its oil, bans half its population from driving. Saudi
Arabia's conservative leadership has always justified this
ban, and the nation's broader gender apartheid, on the
grounds that Saudi society is not "ready" for women to
have more rights. In Saudi Arabia and other dictatorial
regimes, such excuses are used not just to dismiss calls
for change, but also to frame any small concessions

toward women's rights as bold and progressive measures against society's supposed unreadiness. This is nonsense and must be called out as such. There is nothing "exceptional" about Saudi Arabia, and the country's blatant misogyny should not be given any leeway. Rather, Saudi Arabia is exceptional in its degree of discrimination against girls and women.

The Saudi royal family, by wrapping themselves in Islam and presenting themselves as Islam's guardians—the king is known as the "Custodian of the Two Holy Mosques" (the mosques in Mecca and Medina)—maneuvers to make any criticism of them a criticism of Islam. Ever since Abdul Ibn Saud united tribes to create the country named after his family (which has been under the absolute rule of his sons ever since), the royal family has been locked in a deal with the clerics in which the former has free rein over foreign policy and oil wealth while the latter own domestic hearts and minds. There have been conflicts now and then between those two poles of power and influence—especially over a university endorsed by the king that has the only campus in the kingdom that is not gender-segregated, much to the chagrin of the ultraconservative clerics. But as much as it portrays itself to its foreign allies as the more "reasonable" element, the royal family understands very well that "Society is not ready" is only an excuse to brush away criticism of the country's abysmal women's rights record. The royal family also knows it can always count on its allies' silence, due to oil exports, billions of dollars in arms and business deals, and the reluctance of Muslims, especially those belonging to the Sunni sect of Islam, to criticize it. Why else did the Saudi Olympic team show up at one Olympics after another (until the summer 2012 Games) with not a single woman representing the kingdom? (Meanwhile, the Olympic committee banned the Afghan team for discrimination against women during Taliban rule.)

The Saudi excuse was always that girls in the kingdom were simply not allowed to take part in sports, and for too long the world and, most shamefully, the International Olympic Committee—whose charter bans all forms of discrimination—accepted this. Why were girls and women barred from sports in the kingdom? Because ultraconservative clerics deemed women's sports sinful.

If you're wondering how sports could be sinful, look no farther than a 2006 book by the cleric Mohammed al-Habdan. "This [sports for women] is exactly what the disbelievers in the West want," he wrote. "Their plan is to lure Muslim women out of their homes and subsequently out of their headscarf too."

It gets worse: apparently, women's sports are not only a Western plot, but also a gateway to Sapphic temptation. Habdan writes that girls might become attracted to one another after seeing classmates in tight leotards and tops. That is why, says Habdan, "good" Saudi girls do not disrobe outside their homes.

This hypersexualization of girls and women is all too common among the kingdom's ultraconservative clerics and says more about them than about their country's female population.

Twenty-six women participated in Egypt's team at the 2008 Beijing Olympics. I was delighted to see a woman carrying the flag for the Bahraini team, and another for the team from the UAE—the first woman ever to represent her country at the Olympics. Sheikha Maitha bint Mohammed bin Rashid, the twenty-eight-year old who carried the flag for the UAE, competed in tae kwon do. During the opening ceremony, she wore a black headscarf and abaya, although she does not veil when she competes. In contrast, the women on the Algerian team wore skirts and high heels.

A few days before the Beijing opening ceremony, the Saudi women's rights activist Wajeha al-Huwaider posted a video on YouTube protesting the ban on women's sports in her country. Others challenged the ban by playing underground soccer and basketball and learning to ride horseback. In 2008, Saudi religious authorities banned an all-women's marathon and a soccer match, but the Jeddah United women's basketball team made public appearances as part of their fight against that ban. They risked state anger but were determined to be recognized.

All these efforts put enough pressure on the IOC to make it force Saudi Arabia's hand. The kingdom sent two female athletes to the London Games in 2012. Ultraconservatives launched a vicious campaign against the two women on social media, calling them whores—just as the regime's clerics did with the women who dared to drive in 1990—and using the hashtag "prostitutes of the Olympics" on Twitter and other social media. No Saudi television channel broadcast their participation in the games.

Before Wojdan Ali Seraj Abdulrahim Shahrkhani could even compete, her headscarf became the object of a tug-of-war among Olympic organizers, Saudi officials, and the International Judo Federation. Judo officials had initially ruled out competition in a headscarf, saying it could be dangerous because of chokeholds and aggressive grabbing techniques. The Saudi officials, apparently to save face with hard-liners back home for having allowed women to compete at all, insisted that Shahrkhani compete wearing a headscarf. Olympic organizers fought back, trying to overcome their reputation for being too soft in the past on Saudi misogyny.

How small all these officials seemed in comparison to the young woman carrying the ambitions of millions on her shoulders! In the end, she wore a modified hijab—it looked like a black cap. Yet even that was not enough for Saudi hard-liners, who said she was "dishonoring" herself by fighting in front of male referees and judges.

You see—it's not about covering our hair or about "modesty." It's about controlling women's bodies, and to maintain this control, hard-liners will always move the goalposts to our disadvantage.

Shahrkhani was a blue belt judoko competing at the Olympics, for which a black belt is requisite, but she was given an exception. Women in Saudi Arabia cannot qualify for international competitions because they cannot enter national trials in the kingdom because of the sporting ban. In the end, when she finally competed, Shahrkhani lost in just eighty-two seconds, to a much more experienced competitor from Puerto Rico, Melissa Mojica.

The other Saudi competitor, Sarah Attar, at nineteen, was just a year older than Shahrkhani. A U.S.–Saudi citizen who lives in the United States, where she belonged to her university's track team, Attar trained as a long-distance runner, but because she was not among the world's elite, organizers had her compete in the 800 meter.

Like her compatriot in the judo competition, Attar was warmly received by the crowd, which gave her a standing ovation even though she came in last. Like Shahrkhani, Attar was very aware that she was making history.

"This is such a huge honor and an amazing experience, just to be representing the women," Attar told the Associated Press. "I know that this can make a huge difference . . . For women in Saudi Arabia, I think this can really spark something to get more involved in sports, to become more athletic," she said. "Maybe in the next Olympics, we can have a very strong team to come."

In the United States, Attar would run in shorts and a tank top. At the London Games, she was covered from head to toe—a headscarf tucked into a long-sleeve jacket and full-length trousers. Competing against the world's top athletes, who were dressed in the most aerodynamic running gear available, Attar was surely hampered by her baggy clothes. They were a far cry from her running gear in the United States and left her looking visibly uncomfortable in the London heat.

As if these young women's lack of experience and the tremendous scrutiny placed on them were not enough, the kingdom's conditions that they must "comply with Sharia" made a mockery of their participation. Instead of shaming the kind of cleric who would warn that girls' sports encourage lesbianism, instead of shaming the online bullies who called these two Olympians "whores," the Saudi regime instead shames women—when it should be celebrating them. Saudi Arabia sent no women to the September 2014 Asian Games in South Korea.

In May 2013 the ban on sports in private girls' schools in Saudi Arabia was lifted, on the condition that students adhere to "decent dress" codes and the rules of Sharia. Education Ministry spokesman Mohammed al-Dakhini was quoted by the Saudi Press Agency (SPA) as saying that the lifting of the sports ban "stems from the teachings of our religion, which allow women such activities in accordance with Sharia." Yet Wajeha al-Huwaider had already made exactly that point—that Islam encouraged women to play sports and that women at the time of the Prophet did so—and al-Huwaider was routinely called an extremist.

The greater test will come with government schools. The regime has quietly tolerated sports in private schools. In April 2014, the SPA reported that the Shura Council had asked the Ministry of Education to look into including sports for girls in state-run schools, again with the condition that the schools conform to Sharia rules on dress and gender segregation. Reuters reported that conservatives staged a rare protest outside the Royal Court in the capital, Riyadh, against such "Westernizing" reforms. What is "Westernizing" about sports for girls? As with the hijab, conservatives invoke a false cultural dialectic to hide the real nature of the struggle.

Participation in sports must be a right for all girls in Saudi Arabia, not just those whose families can afford to send them to private schools that cushion them somewhat from their country's "exceptionalism." The wealthy often—though not always—are protected from some kinds of misogyny, and the disadvantaged, the most marginalized, and the most vulnerable are often the ones who feel misogyny most painfully.

———

The restrictions on sports and driving are both princi-
pally about one thing: mobility. Saudi women have multiple problems to contend with, but no other issue so
acutely dramatizes their captivity under the regime.

A year before the London Olympics, Manal al-Sharif
was jailed for nine days for driving a car, with her brother
in the passenger seat, and posting a video of this infrac-
tion on YouTube. A single mother with a toddler, she
was arrested after police swooped in on her apartment as
if to capture a terrorist.

At a conference in Cairo where both she and I presented, al-Sharif spoke of another single mother whom
she had met after her arrest. The woman, a mother of two
teenage girls, pleaded with Manal to teach her daughters
to drive so that they could go to school and run errands,
because the mother could not afford a driver and her ex-
husband did not pay her child support or alimony.

Al-Sharif's May 2011 driving campaign, largely organized online, brought out dozens of women who simi-
larly uploaded videos to YouTube of themselves driving.
Several of them offered to teach their countrywomen
how to drive. Some drivers made it home without a problem. Others were arrested, to be released only after their
fathers had signed a pledge that their daughters would
not drive again. All these women had earned their driver's
licenses outside Saudi Arabia, but were forbidden to use
them in the kingdom.

Al-Sharif told reporters that the storm begins with

just one raindrop and argued that the kingdom cannot forever keep at bay the hurricane of women's rights. Conservatives found al-Sharif's storm to be such a threat that she was eventually hounded out of her job at one of the largest oil companies in the world and had to leave Saudi Arabia for Dubai.

In October 2013, two years after Manal al-Sharif's arrest, about sixty Saudi women got behind the wheel. A smaller number of them were detained this time. Interestingly, in a change of tack by the state, two men, including a columnist, were jailed for a few days because of their support for the women's driving campaign. With this protest, the regime had to acknowledge what it had always denied: that it wasn't society that was "not ready" for female drivers. For years, especially in more remote areas, Saudi women have been driving. Some women dress as men to escape scrutiny. Others drive only in emergencies, for example, to rush a relative to the hospital. Others drive just for the sake of it. The world has not ended. Their presence behind the wheel does not cause mass hysteria among male drivers, and some women have their male relatives' support. It is the regime and its clerics who are not ready.

Just sixty women drove in the 2013 campaign, a mere ten or so more than in 1990. This is an indication of the fear and internalized subjugation among women in Saudi Arabia. Nonetheless, it is impossible that those who heard of the driving campaign will remain unchanged by it—just as people across the region watching revolutions and uprisings on their television sets and computer screens have been irrevocably changed, whether or not they join the protests.

Sitting in the passenger seat and filming during one of Manal al-Sharif's drives before her arrest in 2011 was Wajeha al-Huwaider, the woman behind the video challenging Saudi Arabia's lack of women on its Olympic team at the Beijing Games. In 2008, al-Huwaider produced a clip of herself driving in which she offered to teach other Saudi women how to drive and recited an open letter to the country's interior minister asking him to lift the ban on women driving.

Al-Huwaider has been a tireless, fierce, and at times lonely warrior for women's rights in Saudi Arabia. Barred from travel and from writing for the local press, she has often been accused of performing "stunts," of being "too extreme" in her feminism, of being out of touch with Saudi Arabia. But it is exactly her "extremism" that hits a repressive society where it hurts most. To be "out of touch" with a society in which women have internalized their subjugation is an admirable thing.

As long as women such as al-Huwaider are fighting, we—that is, everyone who lives outside Saudi Arabia—owe it to them to listen to their demands and amplify them. Neither al-Huwaider nor Manal al-Sharif nor any of the women involved in the three waves of driving protests has ever called on anyone to "rescue" her. They fight against unimaginable obscurantism and misogyny, and their fight is proof that Saudi women are not only ready for change, but demanding it.

It is cowardly and shameful to refuse to acknowledge their fight—as U.S. secretary of state John Kerry did when he visited Saudi Arabia shortly after the 2013 driving campaign. When asked about the women's demands, Kerry said, essentially, that Saudi Arabia had the right to have whatever social order it saw fit. No recognition of the women's fight or courage. No recognition of the outrageous violations of women's rights. If any ethnic or religious group were being treated the way Saudi women are treated, such an apartheid would long ago have been condemned, and Saudi Arabia boycotted, by the United States and other Western nations.

Instead, Saudi Arabia buys its way into international organizations such as UN Women, where it is one of two countries guaranteed seats on the organization's board as emerging donors. Why are countries such as Saudi Arabia eager to join international bodies such as UN Women? Because it translates into clout—membership in a powerful new agency—with very few obligations.

The United States and other Western countries successfully fought to keep Iran off the UN Women board, yet they turned a blind eye to Saudi Arabia's failings with regard to women. This is yet another reminder that they will ignore women's rights whenever it is more convenient to do so. Once again, women are the cheapest bargaining chips.

It's not as if the United Nations were unaware of Saudi Arabia's terrible record on women's rights. After all, who could forget the farce that ensued in 2008 when a Saudi delegation appeared for the first time before the UN women's rights panel in Geneva and absurdly insisted that women in their country faced no discrimination? The most ludicrous claim came when the UN committee asked why Saudi men could marry up to four wives. With a straight face, a Saudi delegate—a man, of course—explained that it was to ensure that a man's sexual appetite be satisfied legally if one wife could not fulfill it. Not surprisingly, the then UN special rapporteur on violence against women, Yakin Ertürk, soon after went to Saudi Arabia on a ten-day fact-finding mission. Ertürk said after her visit that Saudi Arabia needed to construct a legal framework based on recognized international human rights standards, and she criticized the restrictions on women's lives that resulted from the guardianship system. Amazingly, though, she said the ban on women's driving did not come up in her conversations with Saudi officials. Even more shockingly, she said, "If the ban on driving is going to continue, I think there is a need to provide transportation possibilities for people to get

around, especially those who cannot afford to have a car
and a driver. Whatever the preferred norm is in a country, the obligation of the state is to provide alternatives."

Instead of calling out the ban on women's driving, in
the way courageous activists have, the UN Human Rights
Council's special rapporteur on violence against women
gave Saudi Arabia a free pass by suggesting it create alternatives to women driving. Remember, this struggle is
about women's mobility and freedom. By not recogniz-
ing it as such, Ertürk joined the long list of officials and
international bodies who refuse to call out Saudi misogyny and instead allow it to pass under the umbrella of
"cultural differences." By continually caving in to such
cultural relativism, international officials side with the
regime and with hard-line clerics and fail to support the
brave work of local activists who maintain that their
country should not be given a license to discriminate.

In 2000, Saudi Arabia ratified an international bill
of rights for women but stipulated that if there were
conflicts with the bill's provisions, the country's interpretation of Sharia would prevail. So why sign in the
first place? Especially since the Saudi interpretation of
Sharia is where so much discrimination against women
originates—including polygamy, child marriage, re-
stricted access to divorce, and reduced inheritance for
women. Other countries also hide behind such a condition, which begs the question: Why are they allowed to
sign conventions they effectively ignore?

When are we going to stop applauding the Saudi regime for throwing women crumbs that pass as "reforms"? The fact of the matter is that the power of women terrifies the Saudi regime. At least that's how I like to explain its decision to delay municipal elections in 2009.

It started with Kuwaiti women. In May 2009, four women won seats in Kuwait's parliamentary elections. Their victory was made all the more delicious because the fundamentalists who had long opposed women's suffrage lost several of their seats in the Kuwaiti parliament.

The very next day, Saudi Arabia extended the mandate of municipal councils by two years to give time to "expand the participation of citizens in the management of local affairs." By the accounts of several activists, those local councils are useless. They are the result of the kingdom's first brief fling with democracy in 2005. At the time, five women announced their candidacy, but those first nationwide elections were deemed off limits to women by ultraconservative clerics.

Ever since, Saudi women and their supporters continued to hope that King Abdullah would open up the 2009 poll to women. So you can imagine how nervous the royal family got at the sight of four newly minted Kuwaiti women parliamentarians. Saudi Arabia knows too well that Saudi women can learn from their Kuwaiti sisters: in the aftermath of Iraq's 1990 invasion of Kuwait, many Kuwaiti men and women fled the violence by getting into their cars and driving to neighboring Saudi

Arabia, helping to inspire the driving protest of that year.

It remains to be seen whether women will indeed be able to vote and run for office in local elections starting in 2015 or if the Saudi regime will again balk. In 2013, King Abdullah appointed thirty women to the Shura Council, an advisory quasi-parliament, where they now represent 20 percent of the previously all-male body. But the Shura is toothless, and it is unclear how much of its "advice" actually becomes policy. More indicative of the Saudi stance on women in politics is Grand Mufti Abdul-aziz's remark that letting women into politics is "opening the door to evil"—what the powers that be actually fear is opening the door to a revolution in women's rights.

One of King Abdullah's recent concessions to women was the lifting of restrictions on women in some employment fields, such as lingerie shops, where women formerly had to buy bras and underpants from male sales assistants. This was an absurdity almost on par with the ban on female drivers, which results in women who are otherwise allowed to be nowhere without a male relative, having to spend hours alone in cars with male drivers unrelated to them. This contradiction gives the lie to Saudi Arabia's gender apartheid. It is not about separating women from men, much less "protecting" women from men, but about restricting women's mobility, and thereby their autonomy.

Religious hard-liners are making Saudi Arabia a laughingstock. A country that in about six decades built multilane highways across the desert, and is one of the most connected on the information superhighway, keeps its women locked in a medieval bubble—and the world is shamefully silent.

There are more Saudi women on university campuses than men, yet according to a 2013 *New York Times* article, the employment rate of women in the kingdom is a paltry 15 percent. Slowly, fields such as law have opened up to them. In 2013, Abdullah allowed the first women in the kingdom to be licensed to practice law, with the right to represent clients and to own and run their own law firms. Other fields remain off-limits, though—there are no women judges, ambassadors, or ministers, for example. The highest post held by a woman in government is deputy minister of education, which was attained by Norah al-Fayez in 2009.

As Yemeni academic Elham Manea pointed out in a 2013 article, the Saudi labor code decrees that, in adherence with Sharia, "women shall work in all fields suitable to their nature." She concluded that "Saudi women continue to be marginalized almost to the point of total exclusion from the Saudi workforce."

She went on to explain that "both public and private sector require female staff to obtain the permission of a male guardian to be hired, and employers can fire a woman or force her to resign 'if her guardian decides for any reason that he no longer wants her to work outside the home.' In jobs in clothing stores, amusement parks, food preparation, and as cashiers, guardian permission is no longer required. However, strict sex segregation in the workplace is imposed and female workers are prohibited from interacting with men."

Undoubtedly, that women can work in these fields at all is due not to the altruism of the royal family but to the work of "extremists" such as al-Huwaider and al-Sharif, who have fought long and hard to push the regime to make these concessions. The Saudi king and other dictators must understand that they have to catch up to their people, not the other way around. Only sixty women drove in 2013, but thousands watched and surely were changed forever. Some of those considered "out of touch" actually represent the dilemmas of so many—such as Nahed Batarfi, a fifty-year-old divorced mother of seven who holds a driver's license from the United Kingdom and earned a PhD. She was one of the sixty women who drove in October 2013. She had waited for three months for a visa for a driver to enter Saudi Arabia, and was forced to depend on her nineteen-year-old son to drive her and his four sisters to school and work. With her son about to leave for study abroad, Batarfi decided to begin driving for herself, whatever the consequences.

A political revolution has not begun in Saudi Arabia— unlike in Egypt or Libya or Tunisia—but a social one has. There are more Saudi women on university campuses than men. Women have embraced blogs and social media as eagerly as men. Much as young people in authoritarian countries such as Egypt create in the virtual world the space for themselves that does not exist in real life, Saudi women can express themselves online in ways unimaginable in the streets and public areas of the regime and the clerics.

The reason women such as Wajeha al-Huwaider and Manal al-Sharif and their fellow driving activists so frighten the clerics is that they directly challenge the male guardianship system. Saudi professor and campaigner Aziza Youssef told the Associated Press that just before the October 2013 driving campaign, she and four other prominent women activists received phone calls from a top official with close links to interior minister Prince Mohammed bin Nayef. The caller warned them not to drive on the day the campaign had set for the women's driving.

The regime's response to the driving protests makes clear that it understands the threat these women pose. The brave work of these activists is about abolishing more than the ban on driving: it is about abolishing a system of gender apartheid upheld by the patriarchs within and without. "Until [the guardianship rule] goes, all the changes are just a show for outside," Youssef has said. These women are sending a message to the patriarchs in government and the patriarchs at home that they do not need or want their "protection." The social and sexual revolution is unstoppable, and these women will be remembered as its vanguard.

SPEAK FOR YOURSELF

What would happen if one woman told the truth
    about her life?
The world would split open

— MURIEL RUKEYSER, "KÄTHE KOLLWITZ"

finally began to reckon with my own sexuality when I
was twenty-eight. Just as it had taken me eight years to
take off my hijab, it took me a long time to overcome all
that I had been taught about sex and what I should and
should not do with my body. Unlearning cultural and
religious lessons and taboos can involve a radical turning against all that you have been taught. But it can be
just as radical to slowly unchain yourself, working your
way carefully through layers of guilt so that you do not
completely fall apart from exhaustion and loneliness.

I had spent most of my twenties working hard at building a journalism career. I openly identified as a feminist
and wrote as many features as I could on women's rights.
In the summer of 1995, I took a month off work and flew
to China to attend and report on the United Nations'

Fourth World Conference on Women, which produced the Beijing Platform for Action, the most progressive reproductive rights agenda the world has seen. I had wanted independence and self-sufficiency, and there I was, traveling to China alone, dining out alone, and writing alone. I was very good at alone.

I had learned the terminology of sex-positive feminism, I could write about reproductive rights, and I learned the term *sex worker* as an alternative to *prostitute*, yet none of this new vocabulary applied to my life. For someone who dealt with words and exposed what was usually hidden, I now realized that I was hiding behind those words, as I had once hidden behind the hijab, and that I had compartmentalized and separated my personal life from my political engagement. I used words as weapons in my working life, but I never used them to explore or explain the biggest struggles of my personal life: I couldn't even tell people that I'd once worn the hijab. I realize now that, back then, I did not have the power.

Channeling all my energies into work was also a convenient way to avoid marriage, which at the time was the only way I could conceive of having sex. I had avoided marriage because I feared I would not have the strength to fight the religious and cultural disadvantages with which I felt a wife must wrestle. So I shut down the personal and focused on the political—the external aspects of it at least. But, as I now realize, the political will never truly change unless it is accompanied by a parallel fight in the realm of the personal—the double revolution.

Most of the women I knew in Egypt—highly educated, financially independent women—would invariably pay lip service to the importance of placing children and family first, but I did not want to promote the primacy of something that could hurt me or curb what little freedom I had won for myself. Why should I marry if it meant "obeying" my husband? Why should I have to pretend that, as hard as I had worked, once I had children, my family would have to come first?

I have seen several highly accomplished women develop multiple personalities after they acquiesced to the demands society made of them. While a part of them reveled in autonomy and accomplishment, another pushed their daughters to conform to a code of behavior expected of girls and not boys, especially when it came to sexuality and bodily autonomy. This is how our society's values are passed like a baton from mother to daughter. I've seen mothers push their daughters to marry regardless of the daughters' ambivalent feelings, and push those same daughters to go off birth control and have children regardless of whether they and their husbands felt ready. In doing so, such mothers operate almost in a culturally determined maternal autopilot that is antithetical to the values implicit in their own accomplishments.

I'm not saying that all women should forgo marriage and children. But so many women—themselves
unhappily struggling against the weight of societal
expectations—instill in their daughters undeserved reverence for conservative gender roles. We must remember
that these mothers often do this to "protect" their girls,
and that it is unfair to place the full burden of change on
them unless we also dismantle the system that demands
they socialize their daughters thus. Yet this does not
absolve them. If these women—educated and economically independent—do not push against the system, if
they do not recognize the levels of privilege that cushion them, and that this privilege obliges them to push
against cultural barriers, then what chance do our societies have?

This is all to say that at the age of twenty-eight, I reconciled with the idea that I would not marry anytime
soon. I was fed up with waiting, tired of knowing about
sex and its mechanics only from books and magazines.
Just in time—and I took it as a sign that I should finally
turn my knowledge into experience—I met a man I was
attracted to and who would become my first sexual part-
ner. I asked him out, he accepted, and we began to date.
He was a few years younger than me and was not a virgin.
Nonetheless, he was very patient and accepted the pace
at which I explored my sexuality with him. Just after my
twenty-ninth birthday, we finally had intercourse. That
patience is what I wished for the thirty-five-year-old

woman who asked me if she was "normal" and if she would enjoy sex despite her cutting.

I did not bleed. It did not hurt. It was a beautiful experience that put me on a high, partly because it felt so illicit. I wanted to tell someone, anyone, how wonderful it was to feel the kind of intimacy I'd only ever read about, to experience an orgasm with another person and not just through masturbation, and to say that this love and pleasure were things that should never be tainted with that ugly word *fornication*.

Still, despite the thrill I was finally experiencing, it did not take long for the guilt to push through in a drip-drip that was impossible to ignore. I was not free of my upbringing. I was not free of tradition. Like the young men and women during the protests who feared their parents' anger more than they did Mubarak's police force or the military junta, I was more scared to talk to anyone about my new sex life than I was of the state security officers who threatened to jail me when I didn't reveal a source for an article.

The Algerian French physician and author Malika Mokeddem writes of these feelings in her book *My Men*. Her first lover was a fellow Algerian, whose family scuttled their plans to marry so that they could arrange for him to wed someone from his tribal background. "The tyrannical forces of tradition got the upper hand in that love affair, but they also forced one certainty in me: I needed a man who was free," Mokeddem writes.

In my case, it was not the man I was with, an Egyptian, but rather I who was not free. The "tyrannical forces of tradition" got the upper hand over me. He wanted to get married and have children, and I would tentatively agree, only to withdraw my agreement because I could not trust that after marriage he would remain as he was. Perhaps I also did not trust that I would remain as I was. I did not have the energy or the power to fight our cultural and religious baggage surrounding marriage and family. He understood that I would never give his proposals a yes that would last beyond a week, so he ended our relationship.

Despite all that I had achieved so far, despite all the fights and all the feminism, I was not free. I could not do with my body what I wanted without feeling the weight of guilt, culture, religion, and "fornication." How different, really, was I from the women who I thought had developed split personalities—one that reveled in achievement, the other in being the "good girl" who obeyed upbringing and tradition?

In search of a free man, Mokeddem embarked on love affairs with several non-Algerian men. Not long after I broke up with that first lover, the Egyptian, I married a white American. The turbulent two years we spent together taught me that marriage—to anyone, regardless of culture or religion—was not for me, and helped me to understand that a man's personal attitude toward women is more important than his cultural background. Those two years of marriage also sealed for me the issue of children. I learned that I did not want any. I respect and honor the maternal instinct that many women heed by having children, but I was never moved by it, and I am happy to be child-free. I do wonder, sometimes, if I had had a daughter, how I would have brought her up. How—when it's taken me so long to unlearn the things I believe are most damaging to the cause of women's liberation and equality—would I have raised my daughter to disobey?

Having resolved through my own trial and error the issue of marriage and children, I still had to reckon with the men of my cultural and religious background. I'm forty-seven now and have spent the past eighteen years fighting against sexual guilt. It still lingers at the edges—I have had to fight hard to keep these paragraphs in, knowing that my family will see them and disapprove, but this is my revolution. It is how I am finally reconciling my political and personal and, at last, using my words as weapons in even the most difficult and intimate areas of my life.

When I returned to Egypt for our revolution, I wanted to inhale Egyptian men. There is no other way to describe it. I felt a visceral need to take my guilt-free self—older and better able to withstand the cultural and religious freight under which I had once keeled—and try to find a man who had undergone a similar reckoning. It was well and good to march together, to risk our lives confronting the regime, but what would happen after the protest was over? How would the impeccable politics these men held toward the regime hold up where the social and sexual revolutions were concerned?

Yet so many of the revolutionaries failed to embrace any revolution in sexual politics. I was reminded of the words the Spanish anarchist and resistance fighter Lola Iturbe wrote in 1935 in "Tierra y Libertad," which I first encountered in *Free Women of Spain: Anarchism and the Struggle for the Emancipation of Women*, by Martha A. Ackelsberg: "All those compañeros, however radical they may be in cafes, unions, and even affinity groups, seem to drop their costumes as lovers of female liberation at the doors of their homes. Inside, they behave with their compañeras just like common 'husbands.'"

Amira, a thirty-two-year-old whom I met at the Egmadi event in Cairo, echoed those words when we discussed whether the Egyptian revolution had transformed the home. I asked, is the revolution at home yet?

"I don't think so. Not yet," she said. "Because some of the men who participated in the revolution who act like liberals outside the house, inside the house they are no liberals. They don't even know what religion says. They think, I have to rule you, not, I have to take care of you, support you in your life."

Still, I sought out, and found, men whose love of female liberation crossed the threshold of the home, men whose gentler sides mitigated the violence women faced in public space, where so many of our bodies were hurt and violated. I found men who rejected our society's hypocrisy and double standards over female and male sexuality. I found men who were willing to be comrades in our sexual revolution, who were willing to renounce the privilege that allows them the lazy option of sexual double standards. These men were my allies against any who would leave the revolution outside the bedroom.

It was not an easy search. Some men were still struggling with the chains it had taken me so long to unclasp, and I found myself moved by their personal revolutions. I would remind myself that men also struggled against sexual guilt and a socialization that produced a warped and unhealthy attitude toward women and sex. I believe—and my experience reaffirmed that belief—that girls and women bear the greater burden of this socialization. But in getting to know Egyptian men better, and in sharing my frustrations with the way our culture and practice of religion had filled us with guilt and stripped us of understanding for each other, I learned that our best allies are those men determined to free themselves of sexual guilt and refuse the false ease of gender double standards.

In *My Men*, Malika Mokeddem includes an open letter to her father in which she claims that "to write about men loved freely, in spite of everyone and everything," was the best way to speak against the conservatively religious men—she calls them "the forces of darkness"—who insist on policing women's lives:

> I lay claim to my successive loves, including the "blasphemous" ones. They underscore my freedom of being in this world . . . I insist on doing it. The forces of darkness have followed me here to France. And everywhere in the West they appear in order to deny women the dignity of a legitimate existence. One of their self-appointed great thinkers—a bearded man with fangs as long as the bloody Algerian night—hems and haws on TV screens about the stoning of adulterous women. Their brigades have succeeded in loading this baggage onto the backs of young immigrant girls, putting blinders on them. It is not a given that they will have the last word, Father. There are so many of us whose only religion is the right to equality, to freedom, to love, to sexual choice.

Writing about being loved "freely, in spite of everyone and everything" is too rare a thing in our culture. Very few people in the Arab world are willing to talk about sex that is not between a husband and a wife, and even less about sex that is not between a man and a woman. When an Egyptian friend of mine came out to me as a lesbian, she also explained why—despite long years of activism against the Mubarak regime, despite the ways she'd risked her life and career as part of that activism—she was not ready to come out to her family or the public. I told her I supported her and whatever she felt was best for her at that time, and I was honored she trusted me with her confidence. As a sexually active woman, she was challenging many of our country's most sensitive taboos already, I knew, but with the added risk of the complication and censure that come with having sex with women in an intolerant society. There were so many forces pressing her into silence, into rendering that part of herself invisible.

During my first trip to Beirut, in 2009, I spent my first evening at an event I had never imagined I would attend in the Middle East. At a theater on Hamra Street, two women who openly identified as lesbian took the stage and read, in Arabic and English, from a book about to be released called *Bareed Mista3jil* (Express mail). It was a collection of oral narratives from lesbian, bisexual, queer, and questioning women, as well as transgender people, in Lebanon. The stories involved women from across the country—rural and urban, of different faiths and sects. Some stories were about the difficulty or impossibility of coming out. Some were by people who had immigrated to Western countries only to find homophobia replaced by anti-Arab racism and Islamophobia. One of the passages described the particular challenges that lesbians face in their own culture:

A lot more has been said about male homosexuality than female homosexuality. This comes as no surprise in a patriarchal society where women's issues are often dismissed. And sexuality, because it touches on reclaiming our bodies and demanding the right to desire and pleasure, is the ultimate taboo of women's issues. We have published this book in order to introduce Lebanese society to the real stories of real people whose voices have gone unheard for hundreds of years. They live among us, although invisible to us, in our families, in our schools, our workplaces, and our neighborhoods. Their sexualities have been mocked, dismissed, denied, oppressed, distorted, and forced into hiding.

Bareed Mista3jil was published by Meem, a support community for lesbian and bisexual women formed in Beirut in 2007. "Meem" is the phonetic pronunciation for the first letter in the Arabic word *methleyya*, a relatively recent addition to the Arabic lexicon that literally means "same," as in "same sex," and refers to lesbians. (For gay men, it would be *methli*.) Until the introduction of those words, the only way to refer in Arabic to someone who was homosexual was with slurs, such as *shaaz* ("deviant") or *khawwal* ("fag"). These new words are a reminder of how a culture can be led away from loaded and discriminatory language—and the on-the-ground discrimination they inspire—with the introduction of new words. For a long time we had no word for *feminism* in Arabic, and then *nasawiya* was introduced, helping us to refute the lazy accusation that feminism is a Western import. We need so many more new words in Arabic.

Lina Ben Mhenni, the Tunisian feminist and activist, asks what the word *freedom* means. "When people took to the streets in December 2010, it's true they were calling for employment, freedom, dignity," she said. "I think they weren't really ready to accept that freedom means all freedoms, including women's freedom, sexual freedom, individual freedom; all freedom. They're not ready for such a revolution."

A simple but explosive way to speed the sexual revolution would be the introduction of sex education in our region's curricula. According to a 2007 report from the Population Reference Bureau, only Algeria, Bahrain, Iran, Morocco, and Tunisia include reproductive health in their national school curricula. Currently, the topic gets a cursory (if that) mention in some textbooks, depending on the country you live in and whether you go to a state-funded or a private school. Even in countries that do have sex education, teachers will often be too embarrassed to teach that section and will assign it as something students must read by themselves. Also, parents in some countries have complained that they don't want their children, especially their daughters, to be taught anything about sex.

Most parents in the region are also extremely reluctant to discuss reproduction with their children. According to a 2006 survey in Algeria by the Pan Arab Project for Family Health, 95 percent of male respondents and 74 percent of female respondents learned about puberty on their own, without instruction from parents or teachers.

So where do our young men and women get information about sex? Nowadays, there is at least the Internet and pornography. But depending on what kind of porn they watch, viewers could be imprinted with degrading gender stereotypes and develop an understanding of sex that places male desire and pleasure at the center of sexual encounters.

Many young people learn about sex, love, and married life from television and radio, particularly from talk shows in which clerics (of wildly varying degrees of qualification) answer questions from viewers. Sex and relationship questions are common on these programs, but the clerics inevitably address the topics with sanctimony and misinformation, and address taboo topics (contraception, homosexuality, and extramarital sex) not at all. (To get an idea of the kind of "advice" that awaits women callers, recall my father's anecdote about the cleric who asked an abused wife what she'd done to merit her beatings.)

Without sex education that presents sex as a positive experience—and that mitigates taboo and "dirty" associations—and without easy access to contraceptives or even basic information about birth control, sex will continue to pose a great danger to the most vulnerable in our societies: girls and women.

A physician who specializes in obstetrics and gynecology in Cairo told me that many of her patients in both her university hospital clinic (lower-income patients) and private practice (more affluent patients) present symptoms of sexual frustration but are unable to say so boldly and clearly. When she suggests exercises the women can do with their husbands, most women say they would rather die than propose them. The women worry that their husbands will think they're questioning their virility or, even worse, that the men will believe the exercises are not from a doctor but rather from previous sexual experiences, meaning the women were not virgins when they married. In a culture that enshrines domestic violence, women risk chastisement, beating, and even death by beginning such discussions.

Ironically, due to the extreme difficulty that women face when speaking out, it is a male poet who has best expressed the desires and frustrations of Arab women. The Syrian poet Nizar Qabbani (1923–1998) skewered Arab societies for their hypocrisy and double standards when it came to the upbringing of boys and girls, and the disparity in the freedom to love and to desire they were allowed as they matured. Qabbani's older sister committed suicide to avoid marrying a man she did not love, and many have theorized that this ignited the poet's lifelong attempt to give voice to women's subjectivities, women's passions.

"Qabbani was not embracing fashionable causes when

he began his concentrated attack on the way women were induced, through a narrow conservative education, to deny their own humanity," writes Salma Khadra Jayyusi in her introduction to *On Entering the Sea: The Erotic and Other Poetry of Nizar Qabbani*. "Qabbani's superior achievement, however, is that he not only attacked political coercion, but aimed his well-honed pen at the most sacrosanct taboos in Arab traditional culture: the sexual . . . He called for the liberation of both body and soul from the repressive injunctions imposed upon them throughout the centuries, awakening women to a new awareness of their bodies and their sexuality, wrenching them away from the taboos of society, and making them aware of its discriminatory treatment of the sexes, of its inherent cruelty."

I am a huge fan of Qabbani's poetry. But where is our female Qabbani?

She existed once. One book introduced me to the great female poets of desire in Arabic: *Classical Poems by Arab Women: A Bilingual Anthology*, compiled and translated by Abdullah al-Udhari. Moris Farhi, writing for the website Poetry Magazines, praised *Classical Poems* as follows:

> I cannot think of a collection that exclusively features women who boldly refuse to be voiceless in a world where the male hegemonic psychosis, in various rabid

modes, seeks to enslave and usurp them . . . This is a collection wherein women . . . declare, freely and proudly, their equality with men . . .

It not only includes poetry from the Jahiliyya period (the period before the advent of Islam which Muslim scholars and historians invariably—and wrongly—dismiss as a period of chaos and ignorance and, therefore, of no historical significance), but also from the seminal periods which established Islam as a vibrant, major religion: the Umayyad, Abbasid and Andalusian periods.

The collection's range of female poets from radically different eras is extraordinary, as is how fearlessly they speak about their desires. From the Umayyad Caliphate (603–750 CE), there is Dahna bint Mashal as she reprimands her husband:

Lay off, you can't turn me on with a cuddle, a kiss or
    scent.
Only a thrust rocks out my strains until the ring on
    my toe falls on my sleeve . . .

And Bint al-Hubab boasting of her adultery:

Why are you raving mad, husband, just because I love
    another man?

Go on, whip me, every scar on my body will show the
pain I cause you.

From the Abbasid period (750–1258 CE), here is
Safiyya al-Baghdadiyya:

I am the wonder of the world, the ravisher of hearts
and minds.
Once you've seen my stunning looks, you're a fallen
man.

And I'timad Arrumaikiyya (eleventh century), who
implores her lover with no compunction:

I urge you to come faster than the wind to mount my
breast and firmly dig
and plough my body, and don't let go until you've
flushed me thrice.

What we've lost since the words of these bold and
proudly desirous women! Conservatives will always
charge that the language we use to frame our bodily desires and integrity is "Western" and blasphemous. But
there has always been a language of female desire and
female pride in Arabic; it is ours to reclaim.

There are also words we must remove from the Arabic lexicon on sex. It is time to stop using *girl* for females
who haven't had sex and *woman* for those who have.

Even if the sad reality is that our societies do still believe that it is a man and his penis that make us into women, we must change the language to inspire a change in attitude. That *girl/woman* distinction has ramifications beyond male sexual bluster. Rape laws are harsher in their punishment of the sexual violation of a "girl" than of a "woman," treating a virgin and her genitals as a prize to be guarded for the right man's arrival. The Moroccan penal code, for example, provides for harsher sentences if rape and "indecent assault" result in a woman losing her virginity. In its report on bias in Morocco's penal code, Amnesty International says that the punishment for the rape of a woman is ten to twenty years in prison, unless the woman does not lose her virginity as a result of the assault, in which case the sentence is five to ten years.

We also must have a reckoning with the word *fornication*. In the poorer countries of the region, the average age of marriage has been rising steadily as fewer people are able to afford a home of their own or any of the other expenses associated with marriage. As more and more young people delay marriage, the blanket prohibition on extramarital sex in the Muslim world will be challenged. Do we want a society where lovers marry just to be able to have sex? What if the man and woman who wait until marriage have no sexual chemistry? These questions are forcing themselves on our societies, and only an honest and bold discussion and a willingness to break with tradition, be it Islam or Christianity, will help us find answers.

I am not naïve enough to think that "fornication" will disappear as a concept or as a sin from either the Muslim or Christian way of life in our region. I am instead calling for a pragmatic approach to sexuality that would allow consenting adults who choose to have sex with other consenting adults the freedom to do so, with the knowledge and birth control they require to do so safely. That freedom to choose will not infringe on the freedom to choose to wait until marriage, if that is what you want. The more freedom we have, the more choices available to people. The fewer freedoms we have, the faster hypocrisy will eat away at the heart of our society.

A certain amount of privacy is necessary for autonomy, and privacy is a rare commodity in countries where the patriarch outside and the patriarch at home are constantly on your back, policing your behavior and setting curfews. Most women and men in the region live with their parents until they get married. So where can they find a private place if they want to have sex? Not at a hotel, because most hotels in Egypt demand a copy of a marriage certificate if an Egyptian checks in with someone from the opposite sex. (Ironically, this can sometimes make it easier to have same-sex relations; if you share a room with another woman, no one is likely to suspect your motivations.) In fact, in most countries in the region, including Lebanon, Morocco, and even Tunisia, a man and a woman who want to share a hotel room can be required to produce a marriage certificate. In Lebanon, though it is not legally forbidden, an unmarried couple may be prevented from booking a hotel room under family laws. In other countries, such as Saudi Arabia, an unmarried, unaccompanied woman cannot even check into a hotel alone, never mind with a man who is not her husband.

So where do young people in love go? Cairo has become famous for the shy couples who line the bridges and sidewalks that overlook the Nile, holding hands or sometimes braving bolder moves, yet always facing the Nile, with their backs to the traffic, as if by turning away they are guaranteed a modicum of privacy. It breaks my heart to see these young men and women trying to find their way to what their hearts and bodies want, despite social and religious and political pressures of the most suffocating kind.

A car is the main alternative to a room of one's own, but only for those who can afford one. From those bold enough to share sexual anecdotes, you will often hear cars described as bastions of privacy and sexual exploration. But the streets of big cities such as Cairo are notoriously crowded, so backseat activities can result in jail sentences. In 2012, a former Egyptian parliamentarian—from the Salafi sect, vehement in its condemnation of extramarital sex—received a one-year suspended sentence and a fine of 1,000 Egyptian pounds after he was arrested when police found him "performing sexual acts" in a car on a deserted road with a young woman who, according to some reports, was just sixteen. (Other reports said she was twenty-two.) The former parliamentarian had told the police that she was his niece. The young woman received a suspended six-month sentence and was ordered to pay a fine of 500 EGP.

In Morocco, public displays of affection have riled the regime. In June 2012, Khadija Riyadi, head of the Moroccan Association for Human Rights, alongside other activists, called for the removal of Article 490 of the Moroccan penal code, which punishes those caught having sex outside marriage even if they are consenting adults. Article 490 states: "All persons of the opposite sex who are not related by marriage, and have sexual relations with each other, are punishable by imprisonment for one month to one year." It is followed by Article 491, which concerns adultery: "Any married person convicted of adultery is punishable by imprisonment for one to two years; prosecution is pursued only on a complaint from the offended spouse."

According to the NGO Freedom House, in cases involving sex outside marriage, a conviction can be based on only eyewitness testimony or a confession by one of the accused. The bias against women that Morocco's penal code encourages is more obvious when you take into account how much the law values a man's word over a woman's.

"In the absence of formal evidence or a flagrant case, the man's statement is always believed over the woman's," a representative of the Democratic League for Women's Rights, a Moroccan NGO, told the magazine *MarocHebdo* in 2011. "Many women are therefore accused of adultery simply because they were one-on-one at home with a man other than their husband or even in a public place. Without a witness, if they are unable to prove that their relationship with that man is purely professional and void of any sexual connotation, they do not escape justice."

Riyadi and her fellow activists began the public campaign to change Article 490 after they met with Morocco's minister of solidarity, women, family, and social development, Bassima Hakkaoui, the only woman in the Islamist government elected in 2011. Hakkaoui led the efforts to repeal Article 475, which absolves a rapist who marries his victim. The success of these efforts inspired Riyadi to fight against Article 490.

"Criminalizing sexual relations between consenting adults—regardless of their marital status—violates the right to privacy and to free expression. This provision also deters victims of rape from filing a complaint, because they could find themselves prosecuted for sexual relations outside of marriage," said Hassiba Hadj Sahraoui, Middle East and North Africa deputy director at Amnesty International.

Following the start of the campaign to repeal the law

that punishes extramarital sex, justice minister Musta-pha Ramid claimed that the public was "not ready" for a more progressive approach. He has said that most Mo-roccan families don't want to change existing laws and that they want the option of allowing rapists to marry underage girls to protect "family honor." "These sexual relationships undermine the foundations of our society," Ramid said.

But Khadija Riyadi has reminded us why women like her—too often criticized as "extremist" and "out of touch"—are absolutely essential to the social and sexual revolution. "Laws help to change mentalities. We don't wait for mentalities to change on their own," she told Public Radio International. "We must do something to change mentalities."

Mokhtar al-Ghzioui, the editor of the daily news-paper *al-Ahdath al-Maghribia*, publicly supported Riyadi's call to decriminalize sex outside marriage and said in a TV interview that he would be fine with his mother or sister having consensual sexual relations outside of wed-lock. In response, a preacher named Abdullah Nahari, a resident of the city of Oujda, near the Algerian border, made a YouTube video calling for al-Ghzioui's death. Nahari was then summoned by the local prosecutor to answer to the charge of inciting a crime. Three of Mo-rocco's most prominent conservative clerics, Abu Hafs, Omar al-Heddouchi, and Hassan al-Kettani, all spoke out in support of Nahari on their Facebook pages, thereby publicly backing a death threat against a journalist who had expressed his personal views.

In October 2013 a few dozen Moroccans staged a "Kiss-In" in front of parliament to support three teenagers arrested for posting on Facebook pictures of two of them kissing. The kissing protesters said they wanted to affirm their right to public displays of affection in a country that was becoming increasingly conservative. According to the news website Middle East Online, "around a dozen couples took part in the event, which was swiftly disrupted by a small group of counterprotesters, who accused the couples of 'atheism,' shoved them, and threw chairs at them." The court ultimately acquitted the teenagers, who had been accused of public indecency, but the offending couple, ages fourteen and fifteen, were reprimanded by the judge.

Morocco is often considered more tolerant in the application of its Islamic-inspired penal code because it rarely arrests people who violate the criminalization of sex and alcohol, but this is inaccurate. The regime relies on clerics, who operate with the tacit and sometimes overt support of the regime, to issue the social censure and threats that the regime would prefer not to be seen delivering.

"Legislative reforms to bring Moroccan law in line with international human rights standards are crucial in ensuring that women's rights are protected, but changing the law is not enough. In a society where women do not enjoy an equal status with men, it is not only the law but also deeply ingrained societal attitudes which lead to discrimination," said Hadj Sahraoui of Amnesty International.

Morocco has yet to repeal Article 490. Nevertheless, the protests that Riyadi launched are important in that they have initiated the conversation necessary to combat the silence that surrounds sex. When your culture ensures you cannot figure out for yourself if, where, and when to have sex, it also ensures your silence when sex is forced upon you. It ensures that in the hierarchy of exploitation, girls and women will always be at the very bottom.

When I first explored my sexuality, I felt I needed to keep my personal life a secret; I needed to make my own mistakes and learn my own way through them. This is true for many women, but we must also remember that we need to leave the darkness in order to find one another. In the fight against injustice, it helps to hear truths about women's personal lives. We need to hear not just from the women who speak out about the violations of their bodies and who, in refusing to be silenced about sexual trauma, affirm their survival, but also from the women who speak out about the pleasure of sex, and who in refusing to be silent about their needs and desires affirm their survival as well. It takes a fierce drive for survival to emerge from cultural and religious restraints and say, "I want sex. It is my right to want sex. I celebrate this desire I feel."

If more of us spoke out, what would happen? I know several women who, like me, spent years waiting for marriage to have sex before finally deciding to direct their own sexuality—one at thirty-one, another at thirty-two, yet another at thirty-eight. And there are others who are still waiting.

What if more women spoke openly of their sexual frustration, that same frustration that is used to excuse and justify the behavior of men who grope and sexually violate us on the streets? These personal battles may seem far removed from politics, but what is a greater symptom of gender oppression than a girl whose genitals are cut without her consent and who then grows into a woman who does not know how her own body works, who knows so little about her body and pleasure that she wonders if she is "normal." The more that women are prepared to tell their own stories, the stronger we will be collectively in the public arena.

In November 2011 a twenty-year-old Egyptian woman, Aliaa Elmahdy, turned the tables on our hypocrisy and sexual repression by undressing. She took a photo of herself standing in her parents' living room wearing nothing but stockings, red shoes, and a red hair clip. When she posted this photo on her blog, it was if she'd thrown a Molotov cocktail from the barricades of the personal.

Nakedness and sex, the very things that exercise so many men in the Middle East, became her weapons of political resistance. Our bodies, so often reduced to proxy battle-fields in men's conflicts, can instead be turned into our weapons of choice.

Elmahdy's blog was flooded with visitors, and the vitriol against her came not just from religious conserva-tives incensed by female nudity but also from many lib-erals whom one would have expected to support her act. Instead, these liberals accused her of giving ammunition to the religious conservatives. As if clerics would ever run out of excuses for obsessing over women's bodies! And since when do revolutions allow their conservative opponents to set the agenda?

Some said it was not the time for Elmahdy's audacity. But what are revolutions if not audacious? Some said that her photo would sway Egyptians against the revolu-tion by making them think that it was indeed composed of young men and women doing drugs and having sex in tents in Tahrir Square, as the regime's media claimed. But it is the job of a revolution to shock, to provoke, and to upset, not to behave or to be polite.

Some complained that Elmahdy's body was unat-tractive by Egyptian standards of beauty: that she was not curvy enough, that she had not shaved her pubic hair, and so on. It's laughable that some men want even those women breaking social taboos to fit into their mold of attractive desirability.

Far from being the immature naïf some have tried to paint her as, Elmahdy found the soft underbelly of our hypocrisy—and she kicked. She wrote on her blog: "Put on trial the artists' models who posed nude for art schools until the early 70s, hide the art books and destroy the nude statues of antiquity, then undress and stand before a mirror and burn your bodies that you despise to forever rid yourselves of your sexual hangups before you direct your humiliation and chauvinism and dare to try to deny me my freedom of expression."

Elmahdy received the inevitable death threats and had to leave for Sweden. An Egyptian lawyer filed a motion to have her stripped of her Egyptian nationality, a case that did not go anywhere but that gives you an idea of how much outrage her act generated. All this woman did was take off her clothes in her parents' living room and post a picture of it! You had to go to her blog to see it. She did not stage a naked protest in the street. Tellingly, Elmahdy received more vitriol than has ever been mustered against the sexual violence that plagues girls and women in Egypt.

To put it another way, "Why is violence significantly less traumatizing than our naked bodies?" Lebanese writer Nadine Mazloum asked this question after an uproar broke out over topless pictures of a Lebanese Olympic skier. Jackie Chamoun, twenty-two, was about to compete for Lebanon at the 2014 Sochi Winter Olympics when the photographs surfaced. (The images were taken behind the scenes during a shoot for an Austrian sports calendar, and Chamoun maintained that they were never supposed to be shared publicly.) Lebanon's minister of sports and youth, Faisal Karami, ordered the country's Olympic committee to launch an investigation and "take the required steps so that Lebanon's reputation is not harmed." (His connecting Chamoun's body with Lebanon's reputation reminds me of el-Sisi demanding that Egyptian judges do something about the sexual assault of Egyptian women because "Egypt's honor" was being violated on the streets.) He even suggested that Chamoun's father was happy with the investigation. Patriarchs are often of one mind!

Chamoun's pictures, and the minister's demand for an investigation, appeared a week after Manal Assi's husband beat her to death in Beirut. Nadine Mazloum's question juxtaposed the different reactions to violence and nudity in her country. Luckily for Chamoun, several newspapers chided the minister, and a social media campaign called StripForJackie surfaced, including pictures of women and men posing almost nude while holding signs supportive of the skier. On its Facebook page, the movement expressed its intention to highlight that "some women are beaten or killed, others are raped, and the media shifts their attention to a confident talented beautiful woman who represents her country at the Olympic Games."

Lebanon is not as liberal as it often is said to be—

Chamoun acknowledged this when she apologized: "I want to apologize to all of you, I know that Lebanon is a conservative country and this is not the image that reflects our culture. I fully understand if you want to criticize this," she wrote in a statement posted to her Facebook page the day after the scandal erupted. "Now that I'm at the Olympic Games, these photos that I never saw before are being shared. It is sad. All I can ask to each of you who saw this, is to stop spreading it, it will really help me focusing on what is really important now: my trainings and race."

It was sad to see Chamoun apologize—Elmahdy did not apologize—but it was heartwarming to see some Lebanese defend her. There was no equivalent StripForAliaa on social media in Egypt, despite the fact that Elmahdy deliberately posed nude as a political act. The closest act of solidarity with Aliaa Elmahdy's nude photograph that I've seen, although it was not meant as such, was a work of art called *Tank Girl*, by the Egyptian artist Nadine Hammam. The artwork shows a woman in a pink bikini top straddling a pink tank, the gun of which sprouts pink rats—an ejaculation of sorts. The piece is surrounded by the words "Go Love Yourself."

I saw Hammam's *Tank Girl* as a direct critique of the military junta and, by extension, Egyptian society's fear of women's sexuality as expressed in the "virginity tests" and the assault on the woman who became known as "Blue Bra Girl."

Instead of Blue Bra Girl on the ground and at the mercy of soldiers stomping on her chest, Hammam has placed the tank, that most robust of military symbols, at the mercy of "Pink Bra Girl." Instead of being forcibly spread for a military doctor to conduct a "virginity test," Hammam's Pink Bra Girl's legs are wide open as a way to control the macho emblem of the powers that be in our country. With its implied "Go Fuck Yourself" and the rats ejaculating out of the gun/phallus, Hammam's piece also seems to be saying something similar to Elmahdy's use of nudity: that the female form is, in and of itself, a site of dissent and provocation. Elmahdy had enraged men scurrying to and fro and back again to her website, in both horror and endless fascination; Hammam had rats scurrying out of a tank's gun, in horror but also as a sign of their titillation and climax at her provocation.

In *Talking Back: Thinking Feminist, Thinking Black*, bell hooks recognizes that it is in the place between the public and the private where the most hurt can be inflicted:

> I see how deeply connected that split is to ongoing practices of domination (especially thinking about intimate relationships, ways racism, sexism, and class exploitation work in our daily lives, hurt, dehumanized: there that ourselves are most taken away, terrorized and broken). The public reality and institutional

structures of domination make the private space for oppression and exploitation concrete—real. That's why I think it crucial to talk about the points where the public and private meet, to connect the two. And even folks who talk about ending domination seem to be afraid to break down the space separating the two.

This book is my contribution to breaking that space separating the public and the private. I am a product of my culture and my faith. I am the daughter of the taboos and silences from which I fought to free myself. I am the sister of every woman struggling against the oppressive forces that have suffocated our sex lives and made them such minefields, and resolutely and tenaciously fighting against the oppressive forces that have strangled our societies politically. I am the best friend of the woman who marches in protest against the political despots outside and continues that protest against the personal despots inside.

It is the women who connect the fight against oppressive forces outside and inside who will free our societies. We must engage in that fight while boldly breaking down the space that bell hooks speaks of that separates the public and the private. We must do so with our feet on the streets and our words, loudly chanting, "Bread, Liberty, Social Justice, Human Dignity!" This is the rallying cry of freedom on the streets and at home.

Words are important—to fight silence, alienation,

and violence. Words are flags planted on the planets of
our beings; they say this is mine, I have fought for it and
despite your attempts to silence me, I am still here. Just
as important, words help us find each other and overcome the isolation that threatens to overwhelm and to
break us. Words say we are here.

EPILOGUE

I want an Egypt where my daughter can walk in the streets as free as a boy. I want her to experience everything in her life and no one would look at her and say, "You're a girl, why are you doing this?" I want Egypt to be a place where she can climb mountains, play boxing if she wants to, do anything she wants and no one would look at her and ridicule her because she's a girl and not a boy, and at the same time, not to be always told, "May you be a bride." That is not the goal of your life. You have to first be what you are, anything you want to be, and then be a wife and be a mother and everything you want because to be a mother, you have to be a lot of other things to deliver for your daughter.

—AMIRA, THIRTY-TWO, SPEAKING ABOUT HER
DAUGHTER, FAIROUZ, FOUR

Amira is the mother who attended the Egmadi women's self-defense workshop in Egypt. She brought with her Fairouz, who spent most of the event dancing to the music that accompanied many of the exercises, balloon in hand. What kind of Egypt will we leave Fairouz?

I moved back to Egypt in February 2013 to write this book and to work more closely with women there. That year, the Egyptian Women's Union, one of several newly formed grassroots feminist groups, asked me to talk to its members about sexual violence and ways to combat it. The group was actually a revived version of a union launched by the veteran Egyptian feminist Nawal El Saadawi that had been defunct. When the Egyptian revolution began in January 2011, El Saadawi would go to Tahrir Square, where young women and men would congregate around her, inspired by her years of tenacious and determined advocacy for women's liberation.

I interviewed El Saadawi several times in the 1990s, soon after I became a journalist. She would often tell me that her grandmother was right in defining God as "freedom, justice, and love." Those words would come back to me when I'd hear our revolution's chant, "Bread, Liberty, Social Justice, Human Dignity." After Mubarak stepped down, I attended El Saadawi's talks in New York City, where she reminded the audience why she had been jailed under the Sadat regime: "I went to jail so that I could become free."

I was glad to see the Egyptian Women's Union revived and to see young women and men working together on feminist issues. At the discussion I led, I suggested launching a women's support group for consciousness-raising.

It became especially clear why we needed such a group when a nineteen-year-old woman stood up and unleashed her frustrations. "I am full of so much rage! No one can imagine how much rage I am filled with!" she told us. She spat out those words with such force that we could indeed imagine. What a force to harness, that rage!

The young woman—Alaa—told us that she wanted to remove her headscarf but her mother would not let her, and that her father beat her.

"I want to run away. Should I?"

I told her that I could not answer that question for her. But I suggested that she already knew the answer and that she had come to our discussion for a reason. As Alaa spoke, her predicament reminded me of the emotional terrorism to which too many of our families subject girls and women.

Alaa did indeed remove her hijab and leave home, but only for a few months, because she is not yet of age according to Egyptian law, which sets adulthood at age twenty-one. She joined our support group occasionally, and some of the other members marveled at the fortitude she mustered in order to leave home—a huge step in Arab societies.

Rania, a member of the group who was in her thirties, once turned to Alaa and asked simply, "How did you do it? How did you do all of this at nineteen? I just traveled for the first time by myself last year when I was thirty-four!" Rania is the eldest member of the group, and Alaa is the youngest.

It is these conversations and the juxtaposition of experiences and struggles they produce that bring the revolution home.

"I used to believe women were second to men," said Menna, nineteen. "My father loved to control me and my mum. Before the revolution I thought women shouldn't step up. If I go to Tahrir I'll get molested, harassed, everything, so I should stay home. So I did. But me and my mum went and we did everything and I do feel different. Something in me snapped."

"Since I was a little girl, my parents told me, 'You are free to do whatever you want, but no traveling alone,'" said another woman named Menna, twenty-three. "After the revolution, we protesters were belittled. They started saying, 'Why did they go in the first place?' We were there to defend our country. Why should I belong in my home just to serve men when they come back with a triumph?"

Our support group meets weekly. Into our space members bring their frustrations, hopes, rage, and whatever is on their mind, be it a sense of violation at street sexual harassment they endured on the way there, or the triumph of yelling or pushing or hitting someone who dared to intimidate or violate them in any way.

Several of the women related the suspicions of male friends and coworkers about what exactly we do in our support group, which some men fear only encourages a hatred of them. It's interesting that even when just eight or nine women—we keep the group small to allow for intimacy and for enough time for all to speak when they want—meet in the absence of men, men worry.

When I look around at the group I see women in many of the same struggles I underwent a decade or two ago. There is a direct line that connects me to these women.

I see a rage and determination that cannot be contained. There is a fierce battle raging in Egypt, and it's not the one between Islamists and military rulers, the two factions that dominate the coverage of my country these days. The real battle, the one that will determine whether Egypt frees itself of authoritarianism, is between the patriarchy—established and upheld by the state and the street and at home—and women, who will no longer accept the status quo.

We must connect domestic violence, marital rape, female genital mutilation, and street sexual violence, and clearly call them all crimes against women. And just as we stood next to men to overthrow President Mubarak, we need men to stand alongside us now.

At the time of writing, several women are in jail as political prisoners of the el-Sisi regime. As much as I abhor their imprisonment, the detention of women such as the activist Sanaa Seif, twenty, and the human rights defender Yara Sallam, twenty-eight (both jailed for three years for violating a draconian anti-protest law), is a reminder to all that women have been and continue to be a part of Egypt's revolution, which for too long has celebrated the names of its men over those of its women.

Sanaa's sister Mona, twenty-eight, a scientist whose voice became known from Tahrir Square to people all over the world, cofounded No Military Trials for Civilians, which advocates against the use of military tribunals to try civilians in Egypt. Mona and Sanaa's activism has ensured that they have become as known to those who follow our revolution as their activist brother Alaa Abd el-Fattah, who at the time of writing is in jail awaiting an appeal of a fifteen-year sentence for violating the anti-protest law. The siblings are truly the children of their parents, the veteran activist Laila Soueif and the human rights lawyer Ahmed Seif al-Islam.

Protests are not just for boys. Egyptian women have paid with their freedom, their bodies, and at times their lives to stand up to sixty years of military rule and the Islamists whom the regime was happy to portray as its only alternative, the better to scare Western allies into supporting its rule.

We will have a reckoning with our culture and religion, with military rulers and Islamists—two sides of one coin. Such a reckoning is essentially a feminist one. And it is what will eventually free us. Women—our rage, our tenacity, our daring and audacity—will free our countries.

ACKNOWLEDGMENTS

This hasn't been an easy book to write. Sharing some of my own experiences while I was dealing with the trauma that followed my assault was a challenge, but it was made easier to meet thanks to the support and love of many. My parents, Ragaa and Ahmed Tarif; my sister, Nora; my brother, Ehab, and his wife, Abeer; and my beloved nieces and nephews, Danah, Nour, Hanah, and Zein: thank you for your love, which has kept me sane, for watching football with me even if I'm forever Manchester United and most of you are supporters of archrivals Liverpool, for book recommendations, and for helping me see things in ways I had not considered. Your willingness to discuss and argue difficult issues with me always nurtured my feminism and my fight, even when at times we disagreed. I know parts of this book will be difficult for my family to read. I thank you ahead of time. I am grateful for my agent, Jessica Papin: your faith in me lifted me during many difficult days and nurtured this book through its many fits and starts. Thank you, Mitzi Angel and Will Wolfslau, my editors at Farrar, Straus and Giroux. Your patience and clear-sighted handling of my words helped guide me from the fevered initial chapters to the book those chapters became.

There are many friends in many cities to thank—love to all who help me feel at home in the many places I visit. Just a few: in New York City, Dirk Eusterbrock, Janne Teller, Robin Morgan, Gloria Steinem, and Mary Jasmine Yostos, for supporting and feeding me, lending me money, and believing I could write this book. In Cairo: Rasha Kamel, Tarik Salama, Koert Debeuf, the late Bassem Sabry, and Ahmed Ghaffar, Ayman Ashour, Amira Aly, and Yasmine El Rashidi, for endless nights of conversations, Jelly Cola on my balcony, football matches, and mind-saving music and dancing.

Thank you: Sarah Naguib, Ramy Yaacoub, and Mahmoud Salem, for coming to my aid after I was released; Nasser Weddady, Anne-Marie Slaughter, Nicholas Kristoff, Zeynep Tufekci, and all who spread the word about my detention and campaigned for my release; the field doctors who came looking for their missing colleague and found me at the Interior Ministry and tried to help; the activist who let me use his smartphone to send the tweet about my beating and detention; Alec Ross, for responding to that tweet and helping to get me released. And a big thank-you for all who tweeted #freemona and everyone who helped in any way to get me released. I am eternally grateful. Thank you, Dirk, for nursing me after my surgery. H: I'm glad you survived and I cherish the ups and downs, mostly the ups.

A Note About the Author

Mona Eltahawy is an award-winning Egyptian
American feminist writer and commentator. Her
essays and op-eds on Egypt, the Islamic world, and
women's rights have appeared in various publica-
tions, including *The Washington Post* and *The New
York Times*. She has appeared as a guest commentator on MSNBC, the BBC, CNN, PBS, Al-Jazeera,
NPR, and dozens of other television and radio networks, and is a contributing opinion writer for the
International New York Times. She lives in Cairo
and New York City.